AAT

Synoptic Assessment

Level 4
Professional Diploma
in Accounting

Question Bank

Fourth edition 2019

ISBN 9781 5097 8123 2

British Library Cataloguing-in-Publication Data
A catalogue record for this book is available from the British Library

Published by

BPP Learning Media Ltd
BPP House, Aldine Place
142-144 Uxbridge Road
London W12 8AA

www.bpp.com/learningmedia

Printed in the United Kingdom

Your learning materials, published by BPP Learning Media Ltd, are printed on paper obtained from traceable sustainable sources.

We are grateful to the AAT for permission to reproduce the practice assessment(s). The answers to the practice assessment(s) have been published by the AAT. All other answers have been prepared by BPP Learning Media Ltd.

BPP
LEARNING MEDIA

Contents

Introduction

This is BPP Learning Media's AAT Question Bank for the *Professional Diploma in Accounting Level 4 Synoptic Assessment*. It is part of a suite of ground-breaking resources produced by BPP Learning Media for AAT assessments.

This Question Bank has been written in conjunction with the BPP Course Books and has been carefully designed to enable students to practise all of the relevant learning outcomes and assessment criteria for the units that make up the *Professional Diploma in Accounting Level 4 Synoptic Assessment*. It is fully up to date as at May 2019 and reflects both the AAT's qualification specification and the sample assessment provided by the AAT.

This Question Bank contains these key features:

- Tasks corresponding to each assessment objective in the qualification specification and related task in the synoptic assessment. Some tasks in this Question Bank are designed for learning purposes, others are of assessment standard.

- AAT's AQ2016 sample assessment 1 and answers for the *Professional Diploma in Accounting Level 4 Synoptic Assessment* and further BPP practice assessments.

The emphasis in all tasks and assessments is on the practical application of the skills acquired.

VAT

You may find tasks throughout this Question Bank that need you to calculate or be aware of a rate of VAT. This is stated at 20% in these examples and questions.

Test specification for the Level 4 synoptic assessment:

- Accounting Control and Systems (ASYC)
- Financial Statements of Limited Companies (FSLC)
- Management Accounting: Decision and Control (MDCL)
- Management Accounting: Budgeting (MABU)

Assessment method	Marking type	Duration of assessment
Computer based assessment	Partially computer/partial human marked	3 hours

Guidance from the AAT regarding completion of the Level 4 synoptic assessment

	Assessment objectives for the Level 4 synoptic assessment	Weighting
1	Demonstrate an understanding of the relevance of the roles and responsibilities of the accounting function within an organisation and examine ways of preventing and detecting fraud and systemic weaknesses	20%
2	Evaluate budgetary reporting and its effectiveness in controlling and improving organisational performance	15%
3	Evaluate an organisation's accounting control systems and procedures	15%
4	Analyse an organisation's decision making and control using management accounting tools	15%
5	Analyse an organisation's decision making and control using ratio analysis	20%
6	Analyse the internal controls of an organisation and make recommendations	15%
Total		**100%**

Approaching the assessment

When you sit the assessment it is very important that you follow the on-screen instructions. This means you need to carefully read the instructions, both on the introduction screens and during specific tasks.

When you access the assessment you should be presented with an introductory screen with information similar to that shown below (taken from the introductory screen from one of the AAT's AQ2016 sample assessments for the *Professional Diploma in Accounting Level 4 Synoptic Assessment*).

We have provided this **sample assessment** to help you familiarise yourself with our e-assessment environment. It is designed to demonstrate as many of the question types that you may find in a live assessment as possible. It is not designed to be used on its own to determine whether you are ready for a live assessment.

At the end of this sample assessment you will receive an immediate assessment result. This will only take into account your responses to tasks 1 and 5 as these are the elements of the assessment that are computer marked. In the live assessment, your responses to tasks 2, 3, 4 and 6 will be human marked.

Assessment information

- Read the scenario carefully before attempting the questions, you can return to it at any time by clicking on the 'Introduction' button at the bottom of the screen.

- Complete all 6 tasks.

- Answer the questions in the spaces provided. For tasks requiring extended written answers, the answer box will expand to fit your answer.

- You must use a full stop to indicate a decimal point. For example, write 100.57 **not** 100,57 or 100 57

- Both minus signs and brackets can be used to indicate negative numbers **unless** task instructions say otherwise.

- You may use a comma to indicate a number in the thousands, but you don't have to.
  For example, 10000 and 10,000 are both acceptable.

- Where the date is relevant, it is given in the task data.

The actual instructions will vary depending on the subject you are studying for. It is very important you read the instructions on the introductory screen and apply them in the assessment. You don't want to lose marks when you know the correct answer just because you have not entered it in the right format.

In general, the rules set out in the AAT sample assessments for this subject will apply in the real assessment, but you should carefully read the information on this screen again in the real assessment, just to make sure. This screen may also confirm the VAT rate used, if applicable.

A full stop is needed to indicate a decimal point. We would recommend using minus signs to indicate negative numbers (unless instructed otherwise by the task) and leaving out the comma signs to indicate thousands. This results in a lower number of key strokes and less margin for error when working under time pressure. Having said that, you can use whatever is easiest for you as long as you operate within the rules set out for the assessment.

You have to show competence throughout the assessment and you should therefore complete all of the tasks. Don't leave questions unanswered.

In some assessments, written or complex tasks may be human marked. In this case you are given a blank space or table to enter your answer into. You are told in the assessments which tasks these are. **Note.** There may be none if all answers are marked by the computer.

If these involve calculations, it is a good idea to decide in advance how you are going to lay out your answers to such tasks by practising answering them on a word document, and certainly you should try all such tasks in this Question Bank and in the AAT's environment using the sample assessment.

When asked to fill in tables, or gaps, never leave any blank even if you are unsure of the answer. Fill in your best estimate.

Note that for some assessments where there is a lot of scenario information or tables of data provided (eg budget information) you may need to access these via 'pop-ups'. Instructions will be provided on how you can bring up the necessary data during the assessment.

Take note of any task specific instructions once you are in the assessment. For example you may be asked to enter a date in a certain format or to enter a number to a certain number of decimal places.

Pay close attention to the language used in the question. Key words such as 'evaluate', 'justify', 'compare' and 'explain' will be key to answering the question in the most appropriate manner. The AAT website has a useful 'Writing Skills' presentation and quiz (www.aat.org.uk/training/study-support/search) which will introduce you to the various terms used, and help to give you guidance on your writing technique.

If an extended written task involves calculations, it is a good idea to decide in advance how you are going to lay out your answers to such tasks by practising answering them in a Word document. You should attempt all such tasks in this Question Bank and in the AAT's environment using the sample assessments.

When asked to fill in tables, or gaps, never leave any answers blank even if you are unsure of the answer. Fill in your best estimate.

AAT makes pre release material about the scenario in this synoptic assessment available for you to read before you sit it. This will be available on the AAT website (student login required) at www.aat.org.uk/training/study-support/search (refer to Accounting Qualifications 2016/Professional Diploma Synoptic Assessment (AQ2016).

During the assessment you can access this pre-release material, plus other relevant information provided within the assessment, via 'pop-up windows'. Instructions will be provided on how you can bring up the necessary information during the assessment. For instance in one of the AAT sample assessments the following instructions are given:

Scenario and pre-release material

The real live scenario will be available on the AAT website. Please note, it will **not** be the same as the scenario in the sample assessment.

Pop-ups

The pre-release material is made available in every task via pop-up windows which can be opened by clicking on the links on the menu provided.

Other relevant reference material is shown in pop-up windows throughout the assessment. You can open these pop-up windows at any point by clicking on buttons that look like this:

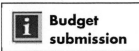

Budget submission

You can open, close and re-open the pop-ups as often as you want and you can position them anywhere on the screen.

Finally, take note of any task specific instructions once you are in the assessment. For example you may be asked to enter a date in a certain format or to enter a number to a certain number of decimal places.

Grading

To achieve the qualification and to be awarded a grade, you must pass all the mandatory unit assessments, all optional unit assessments (where applicable) and the synoptic assessment.

The AAT Level 4 Professional Diploma in Accounting will be awarded a grade. This grade will be based on performance across the qualification. Unit assessments and synoptic assessments are not individually graded. These assessments are given a mark that is used in calculating the overall grade.

How overall grade is determined

You will be awarded an overall qualification grade (Distinction, Merit, and Pass). If you do not achieve the qualification you will not receive a qualification certificate, and the grade will be shown as unclassified.

The marks of each assessment will be converted into a percentage mark and rounded up or down to the nearest whole number. This percentage mark is then weighted according to the weighting of the unit assessment or synoptic assessment within the qualification. The resulting weighted assessment percentages are combined to arrive at a percentage mark for the whole qualification.

Grade definition	Percentage threshold
Distinction	90–100%
Merit	80–89%
Pass	70–79%
Unclassified	0–69% Or failure to pass one or more assessment/s

Re-sits

The AAT Professional Diploma In Accounting is not subject to re-sit restrictions.

You should only be entered for an assessment when you are well-prepared and you expect to pass the assessment. The AAT strongly recommend that you will have completed and been successful at the other units covered in this assessment PRIOR to sitting the final synoptic assessment.

AAT qualifications

The material in this book may support the following AAT qualifications:

AAT Professional Diploma in Accounting Level 4, AAT Professional Diploma in Accounting at SCQF Level 8 and Certificate: Accounting (Level 5 AATSA).

Supplements

From time to time we may need to publish supplementary materials to one of our titles. This can be for a variety of reasons, from a small change in the AAT unit guidance to new legislation coming into effect between editions.

You should check our supplements page regularly for anything that may affect your learning materials. All supplements are available free of charge on our supplements page on our website at:

www.bpp.com/learning-media/about/students

Improving material and removing errors

There is a constant need to update and enhance our study materials in line with both regulatory changes and new insights into the assessments.

From our team of authors BPP appoints a subject expert to update and improve these materials for each new edition.

Their updated draft is subsequently technically checked by another author and from time to time non-technically checked by a proof reader.

We are very keen to remove as many numerical errors and narrative typos as we can but, given the volume of detailed information being changed in a short space of time, we know that a few errors will sometimes get through our net.

We apologise in advance for any inconvenience that an error might cause. We continue to look for new ways to improve these study materials and would welcome your suggestions. If you have any comments about this book, please email nisarahmed@bpp.com or write to Nisar Ahmed, AAT Head of Programme, BPP Learning Media Ltd, BPP House, Aldine Place, London W12 8AA.

Question Bank

Chapter 1 – The accounting function: Accounting Systems and Controls

Task 1.1

Johnson Services Ltd (JSL) is a large company which provides marketing services to small businesses. Each branch performs all its own accounting on a stand-alone laptop and emails results to the two directors once a month. The company has grown quickly and the directors are now concerned that its accounting function and systems are failing to support the business fully. They have approached you for some guidance.

(a) **Complete the following statement that you make to the directors.**

If you want your accounting system to be integrated then you need to

(1) [▼] . A key benefit of integrating the company's accounting system is that you can ensure every area of the business complies with relevant **(2)** [▼] .

Picklist (1):

centralise it
decentralise it

Picklist (2):

laws and regulations
operational objectives

(b) **For each of the following criteria, identify whether a centralised or a decentralised accounting function is better for JSL.**

Criterion	Centralised accounting function	Decentralised accounting function
More economies of scope		
Better communication with business units		
Better placed to produce group accounts		
More economies of scale		

Task 1.2

For each of the following tasks, identify which person will be responsible for their completion.

Task	Responsible party
Preparation of budgetary control reports	▼
Maintain accounting ledgers	▼
Cash management	▼

Picklist:

Financial accountant
Management accountant
Treasury manager

Task 1.3

For each of the following parties, identify their responsibility within a limited company.

Party	Responsibility
External auditors	▼
Accounting function	▼
Directors	▼

Picklist:

Maintain the accounting system
Prepare financial statements for the company
Report whether the financial statements show a true and fair view

Task 1.4

The directors of JSL have decided to have a centralised accounting system with the accounting function operating from its headquarters building. They have identified a number of possible candidates for the role of chief accountant but each candidate has different levels of experience and qualifications. JSL's directors have approached you seeking guidance on the ethical and professional qualities for which they should be looking in their chief accountant.

(a) **If JSL's chief accountant acts diligently they are complying with part of which professional principle?**

	✓
Professional behaviour	
Objectivity	
Professional competence and due care	
Integrity	

One of JSL's directors takes you aside to tell you about a problem encountered by one of the accounting function's staff Kim, an AAT member. A supplier of JSL contacted Kim and asked her to give the supplier a list of JSL's customers so that it could send the customers a mailshot. In return the supplier offered Kim a trip to Disney World. The director only discovered this when Kim told him.

(b) **Answer the following questions.**

Which of the fundamental principles is threatened for Kim by this offer?

▼

Picklist:

Confidentiality
Integrity
Professional competence and due care

What action should Kim take?

▼

Picklist:

She can accept but must advise all the directors
She can accept but must have no further dealings with the supplier
She may reveal the information but must decline the trip
She must refuse to reveal the information and decline the trip
She must resign from JSL

Task 1.5

After identifying a variety of control activities for its accounting system, the chief accountant of JSL has raised a query about what type of security control each control activity represents. They are keen to ensure in particular that the passwords used within the accounting function are as strong as possible, but require further guidance on this.

(a) For each of the following control activities used by JSL, identify what type of security control it is.

Control activity	Type of security control
Passwords	▼
Validation of input data	▼
Archiving	▼

Picklist:

Access control
Integrity control
System control

(b) Which of the following is the most secure password for use by JSL's accounting function?

	✓
Mmmeee	
82s09PQ#	
1357abcd	

Task 1.6

Within JSL's accounting function, the duties of sales invoicing, sales ledger and credit control are separated from each other. The person responsible for credit control, Iqbal Hussein, discovers that two sales invoices have been raised in respect of the same sale. Both invoices have been recorded in the sales day book and posted to the general and sales ledgers.

What is the correct action for Iqbal to take?

	✓
Reverse the duplicate entries and advise the sales ledger team of his action	
Inform the sales invoicing team of the error	
Report the error to the chief accountant	
Prepare a credit note and send it to the customer	

Task 1.7

Iqbal has asked you to tell him whether the following errors would be detected by reconciling the sales ledger to the sales ledger control account.

Error	Detected by reconciliation?
A batch of purchase invoices posted to the sales ledger control account	▼
A pricing error in a sales invoice	▼
VAT on a sales invoice posted to insurance rather than the VAT control account	▼
A sales invoice posted to the wrong customer account	▼
A sales invoice credited to the customer's account	▼

Picklist:

Yes
No

Task 1.8

The chief accountant of JSL has informed you that the company is intending to reduce costs by streamlining the accounting function and reducing the number of staff. They are considering getting Iqbal to take over the sales invoicing and sales ledger functions, in addition to his responsibility for credit control.

Critically comment on this suggestion.

Task 1.9

Iqbal has noted that Tripot Ltd (TL), a customer of JSL, is slow in paying its outstanding debt to JSL. From conversations with staff at TL he suspects that TL is experiencing serious financial difficulties. Iqbal's friend, Josh Jones, is considering selling goods on credit to TL. Iqbal has told Josh that he suspects TL is experiencing financial difficulties and will be unable to pay him.

Identify and explain which of the ethical principles Iqbal has breached by this action.

Task 1.10

Which THREE of the following statements are MOST likely to be found in a sustainability report of JSL

	✓
A discussion of sales figures for the main three products of JSL	
Highlighting the employee volunteering opportunities from a team helping to re-turf a school football pitch	
Reporting on the recycling efforts within the office environment	
Reporting any incidents of money laundering and how the organisation seeks to change its controls going forward	

Chapter 2 – Budgetary reporting: Accounting Systems and Controls/Management Accounting: Budgeting/Management Accounting: Decision and Control

Task 2.1

Budget submission

You have prepared a draft raw materials budget for the coming year for Smidget and Widget Manufacturing (SWP). SWP has four factories across the north west of England, with each factory having a small administration unit which runs the financials and payroll for that site. The main accounting and budgetary process is undertaken at the head office in Southport.

Background information

- The production budget (units) has already been agreed.

- The production manager and purchasing manager have decided to switch to a new supplier.

- The quality of the material will be improved which should reduce wastage.

- The material price will increase.

- Supply should be more reliable which means that inventory can be reduced.

- You have been asked to recommend performance indicators to monitor material costs and to give advice about ownership of the budget.

Draft raw materials budget	This year actual	Next year budget
Production (units)	64,000	67,840
Material per unit	0.4 kg	0.4 kg
Material loss (wastage)	12.5%	10%
Material	**kg**	**kg**
Required for production	29,258	30,152
Opening inventory	1,300	1,242
Closing inventory	1,242	1,000
Purchases	29,200	29,910

Material purchases	£	£
Price per kg	4.80	5.04
Purchases	**140,160**	**150,747**

Write an email to the budget committee of SWP, which:

(a) Suggests **FOUR** appropriate performance indicators (other than cost variances) to monitor raw material costs.

(b) Explains which of the planning assumptions are based on forecasts and why these are not totally within the production manager's control.

(c) Explains the issues in the budget that may indicate a lack of goal congruence between the purchasing manager and the production manager.

To: SWP budget committee **From:** Budget accountant
Subject: Draft raw materials budget **Date:** XX/XX/XXXX

(a) Performance indicators

(b) Forecasts

(c) Lack of goal congruence

Budget accountant

....

Task 2.2

Budget revision

You have submitted a draft operating budget to the SWP budget committee based on Scenario A.

The committee has asked you to budget for an alternative situation, Scenario B, and calculate the increase or decrease in expected profit.

Assumptions in Scenario A

- Material and labour costs are variable.
- Depreciation is a stepped cost, increasing at every 10,000 units.
- There is an allowance for an energy price rise of 4%.

Assumptions in Scenario B

- Increase the selling price by 5%.
- Reduce the sales volume by 10%.
- Revise the energy price rise to 6%.

(a) **Complete the Scenario B column in the operating budget table and calculate the increase or decrease in profit.**

Operating budget	Scenario A	Scenario B
Sales price (£ per unit)	6.00	
Sales volume (units)	84,000	
	£	£
Sales revenue	504,000	
Costs		
Material	201,600	
Labour	226,800	
Energy	17,680	
Depreciation	8,100	
Total	454,180	
Gross profit	49,820	
Increase/(decrease) in gross profit		

The managing director has asked that you respond to his queries regarding the possibility of centralising the administration and financial departments across the business.

(b) **Evaluate the effects on SWP of the impact of centralisation, specifically in terms of the financial, controls environment and decision-making factors.**

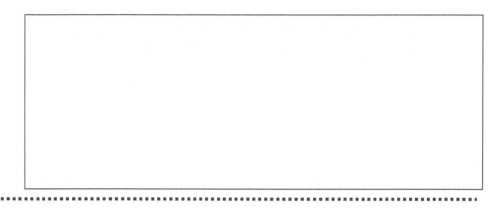

Task 2.3

You are required to complete the monthly operating report below. Flex the budget, calculate variances and show whether each variance is favourable or adverse. The original budget and actual results have been entered.

Notes

1   Material, labour and distribution costs are variable.

2   Energy cost is semi-variable. The fixed element is budgeted at £12,800 per month.

3   Equipment hire is a stepped cost, budgeted to increase at every 30,000 units of monthly production.

4   Depreciation, marketing and administration costs are fixed.

Monthly operating report

Original budget		Flexed budget	Actual	Variance Fav/(Adv)
178,000	Sales volume (units)		192,000	
£		£	£	£
1,281,600	Sales revenue		1,377,000	
	Costs			
462,800	Materials		500,100	
480,600	Labour		516,500	
67,640	Distribution		74,200	
60,860	Energy		65,080	

Original budget		Flexed budget	Actual	Variance Fav/(Adv)
24,000	Equipment hire		28,600	
8,800	Depreciation		8,700	
78,000	Marketing		78,900	
25,600	Administration		24,820	
1,208,300	Total		1,296,900	
73,300	Operating profit/(loss)		80,100	

Task 2.4

Operational review

Review the operating statement shown and the additional information below, and prepare a report by email.

Additional information

The budget has been flexed to the actual number of units produced and sold. The original budget was based on an expected sales volume of 165,000 units which was expected to generate a profit of £227,000.

Sales volume reduced when a competitor undercut our prices. We responded with a 10% price reduction part-way through the year and expected to win back most of the volume in due course.

The budget allowed for a significant amount of overtime working but this was not required when sales volume fell. Material usage efficiency was better than expected and a budgeted increase in material price did not occur.

The original budget was prepared by a management committee and approved by the chief executive. She is concerned that profit is lower than originally budgeted and asks you how she can encourage the management team to perform better.

Operating statement	Flexed Budget	Actual	Variance Fav/Adv
Sales volume		147,000 units	
	£000	£000	£000
Sales revenue	764	735	(29)
Variable costs			
Material	221	212	9
Labour	125	110	15
Distribution	25	24	1
Power	9	9	–
Equipment hire	138	132	6
Total	518	487	31
Contribution	246	248	2
Fixed costs			
Power	15	14	1
Depreciation	16	17	(1)
Marketing	12	11	1
Administration	7	8	(1)
Total	50	50	–
Operating profit	196	198	2

Write an email to the chief executive, in three parts, in which you explain:

(a) The main reasons for the sales revenue, material and labour variances from the flexed budget, and how the sales revenue variance might have been avoided.

(b) How to set and manage a budget to drive improved performance.

(c) How the introduction of standard costing could assist effective budgetary control.

To: The chief executive **From:** Budget accountant

Subject: Review of operating statement **Date:** XX/XX/XXXX

(a) Reasons for variances

(b) Setting and managing the budget

(c)   Standard costing

Task 2.5

Costing queries

Your firm, Ridges Consulting, has been hired by entrepreneur Jack Hamilton, CEO of Hamilton Products Ltd (HPL). Jack does not have a background in accounting and has found himself at a loss to understand certain costing techniques.

Answer the following query from Jack:

What difference does it make to profit if I use fewer subcontractors and hire more employees, thereby increasing fixed costs but reducing variable costs?

Task 2.6

Limiting factors

Jack Hamilton has emailed you the following: 'I've just discovered that a material which is used in three of our products is likely to be in short supply for the foreseeable future. Since we're only likely to be able to get hold of 80% of what we need, I presume we just cut our production of all products by 20%?'

Reply to Jack

Task 2.7

Pricing

Jack Hamilton has called you and asked the following: 'We've just been contacted by a company which is not normally one of our customers. They want us to quote a price for them to buy a substantial quantity of one of our products as a one-off order. We have sufficient production capacity to be able to do this. I'm just not sure of the price we should charge. The variable cost of the product is £187 per unit, the total cost is £279 per unit, and we normally charge £400 per unit. However, if we charge £400 I don't think we'd get the contract.'

Advise Jack on the factors he should consider in determining the price.

Chapter 3 – Accounting control systems and procedures: Accounting Systems and Controls

Task 3.1

Complete the following statement:

Allocating a payment from one customer to another customer's account in order to balance the books and detract from a shortfall is called [＿＿＿＿＿＿▼] .

Picklist:

identity fraud
inflation
reconciliation and review
teeming and lading

Task 3.2

Which of the following are the THREE types of fraud specified in the Fraud Act 2006?

	✓
False representation	
Failure to segregate duties	
Failure to disclose information	
Abuse of position	
Duress and undue influence	

Task 3.3

Identify what, if any, effect each of the following systemic weaknesses in an accounting system will have on reported profit.

Systemic weakness	Understatement of reported profit ✓	Overstatement of reported profit ✓
Overvaluation of inventory at the period end		
Creating an unnecessary allowance for doubtful debts		
Fictitious sales		
Not writing off irrecoverable debts		
Overstating expenses		

Task 3.4

Identify whether each of the following systemic weaknesses in an accounting system could lead to misappropriation of assets and/or misstatement in the financial statements.

Systemic weakness	Misappropriation of assets ✓	Misstatement in the financial statements ✓
Leaving offices where computers are held unlocked		
Failing to maintain an asset register		
Omitting inventory from the annual physical count		
Creating a fictitious employee on the payroll		
Failing to chase unpaid debts		

Task 3.5

Complete the following statement:

Segregation of duties is a type of [_____ ▼] over fraud in the accounting system.

Picklist:

application control
management control
physical control
staff control

....

Task 3.6

You have been asked to review the adequacy of the control in Hansom Ltd's sales procedures. Your review has established the following information.

The company operates an integrated accounting system which includes a sales accounting module. The sales manager is responsible for managing sales activities.

Ordering and despatch:

- All sales, except those for cash, must be documented on an official customer order. The order should state the agreed price, if known.

- Customer orders must be reviewed and signed by the sales manager.

- Large orders must be signed by the finance director.

- Five copies of the order form are printed. Once signed, the original is sent to the customer as an acknowledgement. A copy printed on yellow paper is sent to the accounts receivable clerk. A pink copy is sent to production and a green copy is sent to despatch. The orange copy is retained by the individual who took the order.

- When the goods are completed, production signs the pink copy and sends it to despatch.

- When the goods are sent out, despatch signs the green copy and sends it, with the pink copy, to the accounts receivable clerk.

New customers:

- New customers are contacted by the sales manager. She asks for a trade reference and banking details, and offers credit terms.

- She usually offers credit terms as either of the following:

  – One month from the end of the month in which delivery takes place
  – A 5% discount for payment within 21 days of delivery

  However, terms are subject to negotiation.

Accounting:

- All sales invoices are raised by the accounts receivable clerk. He matches yellow, pink and green copy orders and prepares the invoices for sending to the customer.

- He posts the invoices to the computerised accounting system.

- He answers queries from customers, issuing credit notes when appropriate.

- Most customers pay through the bankers automated clearing system (BACS). The accounts receivable clerk checks the bank account weekly and posts receipts to the ledger accounts.

Identify as many systemic weaknesses in the company's internal controls for handling sales on credit as you can, and explain how each weakness that you have identified could create a problem for the company.

Note. You are **not** required to make recommendations to change procedures.

No.	Weakness	Potential problem
1		
2		
3		
4		
5		
6		
7		
8		
9		
10		

Task 3.7

You have been asked to review the adequacy of the control in Hansom Ltd's payroll procedures. Your review has established the following information.

The company operates an integrated accounting system which includes a payroll accounting module. The accounts manager, based at the head office, is responsible for managing payroll activities. The payroll clerk, based at the factory, performs day-to-day payroll tasks.

The payroll clerk:

- Maintains standing data on employees

- Records each employee's hours at work where this information is relevant and available

- Calculates gross pay and deductions

- Prepares the wages control account

- Prepares the BACS payments each month to employees and HMRC

- Reconciles total pay and deductions in the wages control account

Once a month the accounts manager reviews total payroll cost against budget and investigates unexpected variances.

Which THREE of the following types of control activity are weakest in Hansom Ltd's payroll system?

	✓
Physical controls	
Segregation of duties	
Management controls	
Supervisory controls	
Organisation	
Authorisation (approval) of transactions	
Arithmetic and bookkeeping checks	
Personnel controls	

Task 3.8

Insyst Furniture Ltd (IFL) has grown rapidly in the last two years since its formation and now has a forecast revenue of £10m. The CEO has asked for your advice on the purchases system, which she feels may not be adequate for this size of company.

You have been told the following:

(1)   When materials are required for production, the production manager sends a hand written note to the buying manager. The buying manager finds a suitable supplier and raises a purchase order. The purchase order is signed by the CEO;

(2)   Materials for production are received by the goods received department, who issue a sequentially numbered goods received note (GRN) and send a copy to the purchases ledger clerk. There is no system for recording receipt of other goods and services;

(3)   The purchases ledger clerk receives the purchase invoice, matches it with the goods received note and purchase order (if available). The CEO authorises the invoice for posting to the purchases ledger;

(4)   The purchases ledger clerk analyses the invoice and posts it to the purchase ledger;

(5)   The purchases ledger clerk prepares the cheques and remittances, and posts the cheques to the purchases ledger and cash book; and

(6)   The CEO signs the cheques, and the purchases ledger clerk sends the cheques and remittances to the suppliers.

Identify SIX weaknesses in controls in IFL's purchases system and the implications of those weaknesses.

No.	Weakness	Potential problem
1		
2		
3		
4		
5		
6		

Task 3.9

The CEO of TML has approached you for advice on its payroll system. The company has grown rapidly and now has over 200 employees. There are concerns that the payroll system may not be adequate.

You have obtained the following information:

(1)   On Monday mornings each employee takes a blank time card from a pile and writes his or her name and number at the top. Each day of the week they record their starting and finishing times. The following Monday each department supervisor collects the cards and forwards them to the wages clerk.

(2)   Personnel and wages records are maintained by the wages clerk. From the time cards he calculates the hours worked by each employee and enters them into a payroll program on the computer. This program, using data from personnel records as to wage rates and deductions, produces the weekly payroll and a payslip for each employee.

(3)   The wages clerk prepares a cheque requisition for the total net pay for the week, which is sent to the company accountant together with a copy of the payroll. The accountant draws up the cheque, made payable to cash, and has it countersigned by a director. The wages clerk takes the cheque to the bank and uses the cash to prepare the wage packets. Wage packets are given to the department supervisors for distribution to the employees in their department as they see fit.

(4)   There is no personnel department. Each department supervisor has the authority to engage new employees and to determine changes in wage rates with the verbal consent of a director

Identify SIX weaknesses in controls in TML's wages system and the implications of those weaknesses.

No.	Weakness	Potential problem
1		
2		
3		
4		
5		
6		

Chapter 4 – Decision making and control: Accounting Systems and Controls/Management Accounting: Decision and Control

Task 4.1

Complete the following statement.

The [　　　　　　▾] total variance may be analysed into expenditure, efficiency and capacity variances.

Picklist:

fixed overheads
labour
materials
variable overheads

Task 4.2

Yombo Ltd makes the product X07. The standard and actual results for the month of June 20X1 are as follows.

		Standard		Actual
Production (units of X07)		14,000		13,500
Direct materials	17,500 litres	£28,875	16,800 litres	£106,000
Direct labour	3,500 hours	£59,500	3,650 hours	£65,700
Fixed overheads (absorbed on a unit basis)		£77,000		£79,500
Total		£165,375		£251,200

Complete the following statements.

(a) The standard quantity of labour per unit is [　　　　　] minutes.

(b) The standard quantity of materials needed to produce 13,500 units of X07 is [　　　　　] litres.

(c) The standard labour hours to produce 12,000 units of X07 is [　　　　　] hours.

(d) The standard labour cost to produce 13,500 units of X07 is
£ [　　　　　].

BPP
LEARNING MEDIA

(e) The standard overhead absorption rate per unit is £ [ ].

....

Task 4.3

Statham Ltd purchases 3,700 kilograms of material at a cost of £10,915. The total material price variance is £1,665 adverse.

(a) **Complete the following statement.**

The standard cost per kilogram is £ [ ].

Statham Ltd purchases and uses 200,000 litres of a different material at a cost of £0.55 per litre. The budgeted production was 22,000 units which requires 220,000 litres of material at a total standard cost of £132,000. The actual production was 19,000 units.

(b) **Complete the following statement.**

The material usage variance is £ [ ] [▼].

Picklist:

Adverse
Favourable

Statham Ltd expects to produce 10,000 units of X using 6,000 hours of labour. The standard cost of labour is £15 per hour. The actual output was 12,000 units. 6,900 hours of labour were worked and 7,300 hours were paid at a total cost of £105,850.

(c) **Complete the following statements.**

The total labour efficiency variance is £ [ ] [▼].

Picklist:

Adverse
Favourable

The idle time variance is £ [ ] [▼].

Picklist:

Adverse
Favourable

....

Task 4.4

Bert Ltd manufactures product RPB. Bert Ltd operates a standard cost system in which production overheads are fixed and absorbed on a unit basis.

The budgeted activity is for the production of 28,000 units at a total fixed production cost of £350,000. The actual volume of production was 30,000 units and the fixed overhead expenditure variance was £35,000 favourable.

Complete the following statements.

The fixed overhead volume variance is £ [   ] [▾] .

Picklist:

Adverse
Favourable

The actual fixed production overheads incurred were £ [   ] .

Task 4.5

Randall Ltd manufactures product RTF. The budgeted activity and actual results for the month are as follows.

	Budget	Actual
Production units (RTF)	64,000	67,000
Direct labour costs	£5,760,000	£5,896,000
Fixed overheads	£3,840,000	£3,950,000

Overheads are absorbed on a labour hour basis and the budget uses 480,000 labour hours. The actual labour hours used to produce 67,000 units totalled 536,000 labour hours.

Calculate the following variances.

Variance	Amount £	Adverse/Favourable
Fixed overhead capacity		[▾]
Fixed overhead efficiency		[▾]

Picklist:

Adverse
Favourable

Task 4.6

The following budgetary control report has been provided for Pelling Ltd together with the variances calculated below.

	Budget		Actual	
Production (units)		12,400		13,600
Direct materials	37,200 kg	£130,200	37,400 kg	£112,200
Direct labour	24,800 hours	£223,200	28,560 hours	£285,600
Fixed overheads		£234,000		£221,000
Total cost		£587,400		£618,800

Variance	Amount ✓
Direct materials price	18,700 F
Direct materials usage	11,900 F
Direct labour rate	28,560 A
Direct labour efficiency	Not yet calculated
Fixed overhead expenditure	Not yet calculated

Pelling Ltd normally prepares an operating statement under standard absorption costing principles but the financial director has asked you to prepare one under standard marginal costing principles.

Place each variance into the correct column (favourable or adverse) and complete the table.

			£
Budgeted variable cost for actual production			
Budgeted fixed cost			
Total budgeted cost for actual production			
Variance	**Favourable £**	**Adverse £**	
Direct materials price			
Direct materials usage			
Direct labour rate			
Direct labour efficiency			
Fixed overhead expenditure			
Fixed overhead volume	[▼]	[▼]	
Total variance			
Actual cost of actual production			

Picklist:

22,645
N/A

Task 4.7

Keta Ltd operates a standard costing system and uses raw material C2X, which is a global commodity. The standard price was set based upon a market price of £450 per litre when the material price index for C2X was 120.50. The following information has been gathered:

- The price index increased to 126.525 in June 20X3.
- The raw material price variance for June was £375,000 adverse.
- 12,500 litres of material C2X were purchased in June.

Complete the statements below. In order to calculate your answers, you should split the raw material price variance into two components by calculating the part of the variance explained by the change in the price index and the part of the variance not explained by the change in the price index.

(a) The part of the variance explained by the increase in the price index is

£ [   ].

(b) The part of the variance not explained by the increase in the price index is

£ [   ].

(c) The percentage increase in the index is [   ] %.

Keta Ltd also uses product Z4QX and has collected data from the last few months in order to forecast the cost per kilogram of Z4QX in the next period.

	April 20X3	May 20X3	June 20X3
Cost per kilogram of Z4QX (£)	1,457.92	1,593.66	1,729.40

(d) **Complete the table below to forecast the expected price of product Z4QX in September and December 20X3.**

	September 20X3	December 20X3
Cost per kilogram of Z4QX (£)		

A colleague has calculated the least squares regression line (the line of best fit) for a different product as **y = 24.69 + 2.14x**, where y is the cost per kilogram (in £) and x is the monthly period. June 20X3 is period 41.

(e) **Complete the statement below.**

The forecast cost per kilogram, using the regression line, for September 20X3 is £ [   ].

Task 4.8

You have been provided with the following information for Vocco Ltd, which manufactures a product called Becks, for the month just ended.

	Budget		Actual	
Production (units)		20,000		21,000
Direct materials	80,000 kg	£880,000	83,000 kg	£954,500

The finance director has asked you to write a note to help in the training of a junior accounting technician. The notes are to explain the calculation of the total direct material variance and how this variance can be split into a price variance and a usage variance.

Prepare a note explaining the total direct material variance and how it can be split into a price variance and usage variance. Calculations should be used to illustrate the explanation.

Task 4.9

You have been provided with the following information for two scenarios involving a company which operates an absorption costing system.

	Scenario 1	Scenario 2
Sales volume (units)	120,000	150,000
	£	£
Revenue	1,680,000	1,800,000
Gross profit	600,000	450,000
Profit from operations	275,000	200,000
Capital employed	2,298,400	2,100,340
Inventory	147,950	167,500

(a) Calculate the following performance indicators for Scenario 1 and 2.

	Scenario 1	Scenario 2
Return on capital employed		
Inventory holding period in days		
Sales price per unit		
Full production cost per unit		

(b) Complete the table below for Scenario 3.

	Scenario 3
Capital employed (£)	175,000
Return on capital employed (%)	13
Profit margin (%)	14
Gearing (%)	32.75
Profit (to the nearest £)	
Sales revenue (to the nearest £)	

(c) **Fill in the boxes with the appropriate options to show how to calculate the gearing. If there is more than one correct answer, either answer will achieve full marks.**

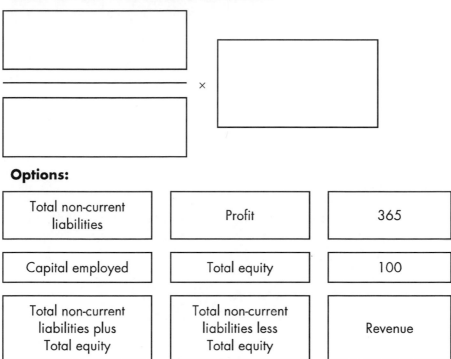

Options:

Total non-current liabilities	Profit	365
Capital employed	Total equity	100
Total non-current liabilities plus Total equity	Total non-current liabilities less Total equity	Revenue

Task 4.10

Alpha Ltd makes two products, Tig and Tag. The following information is available for the next month.

	Product Tig £ per unit	Product Tag £ per unit
Selling price	4,000	4,930
Variable costs		
Material cost (£400 per kilogram)	2,400	3,000
Labour cost	400	600
Total variable cost	2,800	3,600

	Product Tig £ per unit	Product Tag £ per unit
Fixed costs		
Production cost	450	450
Administration cost	300	300
Total fixed costs	750	750
Profit per unit	450	600
Monthly demand	200 units	300 units

The materials are in short supply in the coming month and only 3,000 kilograms of material will be available from the existing supplier.

(a) **Complete the table below.**

	Product Tig £	Product Tag £
The contribution per unit is		
The contribution per kilogram of materials is		

(b) **Complete the following statement.**

The optimal production order for products Tig and Tag is [　　　　▼].

Picklist:

Tag then Tig
Tig then Tag

(c) **Complete the table below for the optimal production mix.**

	Product Tig	Product Tag
Production in units		

(d) **Complete the table below for the total contribution for each product.**

	Product Tig £	Product Tag £
Total contribution		

Alpha Ltd has been approached by another materials supplier who can supply up to 500 kilograms of material at a cost per kilogram of £500. This is a premium of £100 above the normal cost per kilogram.

(e)   Complete the table below.

Should Alpha Ltd purchase the additional material?	Give a reason
(1) ▼	(2) ▼

Picklist (1):

Yes

No

Picklist (2):

The additional cost per kilogram is greater than the contribution per kilogram

The additional cost per kilogram is greater than the contribution per unit

The additional cost per kilogram is less than the contribution per kilogram

The additional cost per kilogram is less than the contribution per unit

Task 4.11

Alpha Ltd is considering designing a new product, product BPT, and will use target costing to arrive at the target cost of the product. You have been given the following information.

- The price at which the product will be sold has not yet been decided.

- It has been estimated that if the price is set at £40 the demand will be 500,000 units, and if the price is set at £50 the demand will be 430,000 units.

- The costs of production include fixed production costs of £8,500,000 which will give a production capacity of 500,000 units.

- In order to produce above this level the fixed costs will step up by £1,500,000.

- The required profit margin is 30%.

- The variable cost per unit is £13 for the production volume of 430,000 units.

- For production volume of 500,000 units the variable cost will be £12 per unit.

(a) **Complete the table for both levels of demand.**

	Sales price £40	Sales price £50
The target total production cost per unit		
The target fixed production cost per unit		
The target total fixed production cost		

(b) **Complete the following statement.**

Alpha should set the price at [▼] in order to achieve the target profit margin.

Picklist:

£40
£50

Task 4.12

You have been provided with the following information for Beta Ltd.

Current position

The price is currently £22 per unit. At this price demand is 150,000 units each year. The advertising costs are currently £500,000 per year. The current factory can produce a maximum of 400,000 units per annum. The labour and material costs are the only variable costs.

Proposed position

The price will reduce to £18 per unit. Advertising costs will increase to £750,000 per year and it is expected that this will increase demand to 300,000 units per year. The factory will still be limited to 400,000 units per year. The labour and material costs are the only variable costs.

The forecast information for each scenario is shown below.

Statement of profit or loss	Current position (actual)	Proposed position (forecast)
Sales price per unit	£22	£18
Sales volume	150,000	300,000
	£	£
Revenue	3,300,000	5,400,000
Direct materials	750,000	1,200,000
Direct labour	900,000	1,800,000
Fixed production costs	600,000	600,000
Total cost of sales	2,250,000	3,600,000
Gross profit	1,050,000	1,800,000
Fixed advertising costs	500,000	750,000
Administration costs	300,000	400,000
Profit	250,000	650,000
Material cost per unit	£5.00	£4.00
Labour cost per unit	£6.00	£6.00
Fixed production cost per unit	£4.00	£2.00
Fixed advertising cost per unit	£3.33	£2.50
Gross profit margin	31.82%	33.33%
Profit margin	7.58%	12.04%
Inventory of finished goods	£350,000	
Trade receivables	£500,000	

Draft a report for the finance director covering the following:

(a) An explanation of why the gross profit margin for the proposed position is higher than the current position, referring to the following:

- Sales volume
- Materials cost
- Labour cost
- Fixed production costs

(b) An explanation of what is likely to happen to the current asset position of the business by considering the following:

- Inventory levels (include a prediction of inventory level based upon the current inventory holding period)

- Trade receivable levels (include a prediction of the level based upon current trade receivables collection period)

To:	Finance director	**Subject:**	Variances
From:	Accounting technician	**Date:**	Today

(a) **Sales volume**

Materials cost

Labour cost

Fixed production costs

(b)   Inventory levels

Trade receivables levels

Task 4.13

Seismic Security Systems Ltd (SSSL) is a rapidly expanding company which sells security cameras to small and medium-sized businesses. The CEO, Teresa Maynot, has asked you to review the sales system, which she currently oversees, and suggest how it should be updated in light of the company's growth. She has provided you with the following information about the existing system:

Sales are made through a team of five sales staff. As they are thought to know the customers best, they are responsible for assessing the creditworthiness of new customers and setting their initial credit limit. Sales staff are also able to make decisions on the amount of sales discount to grant to customers, up to a maximum of 20%, which they then record in the customer's master file.

Sales staff then email the despatch and accounting departments to initiate the despatch and invoicing of the goods. The company's terms of sale are 30 days, and at the end of each month a list of outstanding receivables over 120 days are passed to the sales staff for them to follow up with the relevant customers.

(a) **Suggest TWO new roles which SSSL should recruit in order to improve the sales system. Identify for each role the tasks they should take over and why.**

(b) **Explain TWO potential problems which SSSL might face after recruiting individuals to these roles.**

Task 4.14

Gritby Fish Co manufactures three products – Prawn, Roe and Bass. The net profit from these is shown below:

	Prawn £	Roe £	Bass £	Total £
Sales	100,000	80,000	120,000	300,000
Variable costs	60,000	50,000	70,000	180,000
Contribution	40,000	30,000	50,000	120,000
Fixed costs	34,000	36,000	40,000	110,000
Profit/loss	6,000	(6,000)	10,000	10,000

Gritby is concerned about the performance of Roe and is deciding whether it should cease production of them in order to produce a new product, Codlings.

The forecasted profit generated by Codlings is shown below:

	Codlings £
Sales	90,000
Variable costs	66,000
Contribution	24,000
Fixed costs	16,000
Profit/loss	8,000

Additional information

- The fixed costs associated with the production of Roe are £10,000.
- Directly attributable fixed costs of Codlings are £12,000.

Critically appraise, using numerical evidence where appropriate, whether Gritby Fish Co should cease the production of Roe and start selling Codlings.

••

Task 4.15

Daisy Ltd owns two subsidiaries, Dandelion and Blossom.

Dandelion manufactures bespoke furniture, relying on local suppliers of sustainable wood and Blossom makes a mid-range equivalent, sourcing the raw materials from overseas. Both are sold to local, independent retailers, although customers do not buy from both companies, due to the different target audiences.

The forecasts for both factories for the year ending 31 December 20X5 are below:

	Dandelion £000		Blossom £000	
Revenue	2,200		2,850	
Direct materials	660		784	
Direct labour	440		448	
Fixed production overheads	220		420	
Cost of sales	1,320		1,652	
Gross profit	880	40%	1,198	42%
Sales and distribution costs	520		640	
Administration costs	210		250	
Profit from operations	150	6.8%	308	10.8%

Other information:

- Inventories are of raw materials and will remain unchanged throughout the year.
- All material and labour costs are variable.
- Sales and distribution costs are variable in proportion to the turnover from each factory.
- Administration costs are fixed.

The Managing Director has proposed closing Dandelion. The impact to Blossom's results will be as follows:

- Revenue would increase by 40%.
- Fixed production overheads will increase by £100,000.
- Administration costs will increase by £60,000.
- It is forecast that raw material purchasing costs will decrease by 5% as a result of the closure.

(a) **Prepare a revised statement of profit or loss for Blossom, assuming Dandelion is closed.**

	Blossom £000	
Revenue		
Materials		
Direct labour		
Fixed production overheads		
Cost of sales		
Gross profit		%
Sales and distribution costs		
Administration costs		
Profit from operations		%

(b) **Recommend whether Dandelion should be closed or remain open, give brief reasons for your answer.**

(c) **Give ONE example of a non-financial consideration which the Board of Directors of Daisy Ltd should consider prior to making their decision. State a potential problem for the company relating to this consideration.**

Task 4.16

Connolly Computers Ltd (CCL) develops and licences specialist computer software and hardware. CCL is experiencing increasing competition from rival companies, most of which specialise in hardware or software, but not both. There is pressure to advertise and to cut prices.

You have been provided with the following information:

Statement of profit and loss

| | Year ended 31 Dec | |
	20X3 £000	20X2 £000
Revenue	15,206	13,524
Cost of sales	3,009	3,007
Gross profit	12,197	10,517
Distribution costs	3,006	1,996
Administrative expenses	994	1,768
Selling expenses	3,002	274
Profit from operations	5,195	6,479
Net interest receivable	995	395
Profit before tax	6,190	6,874
Income tax expense	3,104	1,452
Net profit	3,086	5,422
Retained profits	1,617	3,983
Dividends paid	1,469	1,439
	%	%
Accounting ratios and percentages		
Gross profit percentage	80	78
Expenses as a percentage of revenue		
Distribution costs	20	15
Administrative expenses	7	13
Selling expenses	20	2
Operating profit	34	48

The following information is also available:

- In order to try and compete with their rivals, a new e-commerce portal to allow retail customers to buy direct from CCL was built at a cost of £350,000. This was launched in October 20X3.

- The Managing Director decided at the start of 20X3 to focus on sales, and made redundancies, mainly in the financial and customer support areas. New staff were recruited in the warehouse and sales teams, they were brought in quickly and told to 'go out and sell'.

- Budgets are drawn up once a year, and actuals are compared to budget. CCL does not flex its budgets once approved.

- The tax rate remains static year on year.

(a) **Evaluate whether the staff changes at CCL during 20X3 would have impacted upon the performance of the company. Identify any potential issues which may have arisen.**

(b) **Comment briefly on the financial performance of the company for the two years.**

Chapter 5 – Ratio analysis: Accounting Systems and Controls/Financial Statements of Limited Companies/Management Accounting: Decision and Control

Task 5.1

Which of the following is the correct calculation of the working capital cycle?

	✓
Receivables days + Inventory days – Payables days	
Receivables days + Payables days – Inventory days	
Inventory days + Receivables days + Payables days	
Inventory days – Receivables days – Payables days	

Task 5.2

In accordance with the IASB Conceptual Framework for Financial Reporting:

(a) Identify the TWO fundamental characteristics of useful information.

	✓
Understandability	
Relevance	
Comparability	
Faithful representation	

(b) Define the term 'income'.

Inventory holding period ▼

Picklist:

Cost of sales/Inventories
Inventories/Cost of sales × 365
Inventories/Revenue × 365
Revenue/Inventories

Asset turnover (net assets) ▼

Picklist:

Profit from operations/(Total assets – Current liabilities)
Profit from operations/Total assets
Revenue/(Total assets – Current liabilities)
Revenue/Total assets

Gearing ▼

Picklist:

Current assets/Current liabilities × 100
Non-current liabilities/(Total equity + Non-current liabilities) × 100
Profit from operations/(Total equity + Non-current liabilities) × 100
Revenue/(Total assets – Current liabilities) × 100

(b) Calculate the above ratios to ONE decimal place

Return on equity ☐ %

Acid test ratio ☐ : 1

Inventory holding period ☐ days

Asset turnover (net assets) ☐ times

Gearing ☐ %

Task 5.4

Carol Bright, the Financial Director of Poole Ltd, is concerned that the company is not managing its working capital efficiently. She has asked for your assistance in identifying any problem area(s) and for your suggestions as to how these can be remedied.

You have calculated the following ratios in respect of Poole Ltd's latest financial statements and have also obtained each of their industry averages for comparative purposes.

	Poole Ltd	Industry average
Current ratio	5.1:1	2.3:1
Inventory turnover	7.2 times	6.8 times
Trade receivables collection period	63 days	45 days
Trade payables payment period	44 days	51 days

Prepare a reply to Carol that includes:

(a) Comments on whether Poole Ltd has performed better or worse in respect of the calculated ratios, giving possible reasons, as compared to the industry averages.

(b) The steps to be taken to improve Poole Ltd's working capital cycle and any possible problems you think may arise from implementing these actions.

Task 5.5

Abbas Ltd uses a balanced scorecard to measure and control its financial performance. The Finance Director has asked you to calculate certain ratios for inclusion in the scorecard.

The following data is available.

Extracts from accounts of Abbas Ltd	Year ended 31 December 20X4 £000	Year ended 31 December 20X5 £000
Revenue	16,500	17,120
Cost of sales	7,540	8,480
Gross profit	8,960	8,640
Profit from operations	2,060	2,150
Assets		
Non-current assets	5,780	5,060
Inventories	2,450	2,900
Trade receivables	1,870	2,010
Cash and equivalents	30	340
Total assets	**10,130**	**10,310**
Equity and liabilities		
Equity	6,020	7,190
Non-current liabilities	2,590	1,070
Trade payables	1,130	1,670
Tax liabilities	390	380
Total equity and liabilities	**10,130**	**10,310**

(a) **Which TWO of the following statements are recommended perspectives in the Balanced Scorecard framework:**

	✓
Financial perspectives of the company, such as profit margins	
Supplier perspectives, such as the number of supplier complaints	
Customer perspectives of the company, such as number of repeat orders	

(b) **Complete the Balanced Scorecard by calculating the ratios for the year ended 31 December 20X5. Answers should be rounded to ONE decimal point, or whole days.**

Abbas Ltd Balanced Scorecard	Year ended 31 Dec 20X4	Year ended 31 Dec 20X5
Profitability and gearing (correct to 1 dp):		
Gross profit %	54.3%	%
Operating profit %	12.5%	%
Return on capital employed	23.9%	%
Gearing (debt/debt + equity)	30.1%	%
Liquidity ratios (correct to 1 dp):		
Current ratio	2.9:1	:1
Acid test/quick ratio	1.3:1	:1
Working capital days (correct to nearest day):		
Inventory holding period	119 days	days
Trade receivables collection period	41 days	days
Trade payables payment period	55 days	days
Working capital cycle	105 days	days

(c) **Select the ONE correct observation about each aspect of business performance below.**

(i) **Profitability**

	✓
This has been a year of steady, if unspectacular, progress. Although profitability has dipped, the return on capital employed has been kept under control.	
The profitability ratios give cause for concern. The small increase in sales revenue has not improved the gross profit percentage. Operating expenses have increased, reducing operating profit and return on capital employed.	
The ratios give mixed messages. Some have improved and some have deteriorated. Further investigation is required.	

(ii) **Gearing**

	✓
The decreased gearing ratio is due to the repayment of non-current liabilities.	
It is likely that the interest cover ratio has decreased.	
The increased gearing ratio shows that the company has become more risky.	

(iii) **Liquidity**

	✓
Both ratios have deteriorated which indicates that the company is less solvent than last year, however both ratios still fall within an acceptable level	
Both ratios remain quite high, which may indicate that working capital is not being used effectively.	
Some liquidity ratios have improved and some have deteriorated. Further investigation is required to understand whether liquidity is improving.	

(iv) Working capital

	✓
The working capital cycle has worsened. The inventory holding period has improved but the other ratios indicate a lack of financial control.	
There is a welcome improvement in the working capital cycle, mainly due to the change in the payment period for payables.	
The working capital cycle is worse than a year ago because of the increased revenue.	

(v) Overall performance

	✓
Profitability has declined in 20X5. However, the gearing and liquidity measures show an improving financial position.	
20X5 has been a bad year. Profitability has declined and finances are coming under pressure.	
Steady progress has been made in 20X5. The ratios show that the company is being better managed.	

Task 5.6

Explain the possible reasons for the following changes in the ratios of a company from one year to the next:

- **An increase in the current ratio**
- **A decrease in the gross profit margin**
- **An increase in the inventory holding period**
- **An increase in gearing**

Note. You are not required to show the calculation of the ratios.

Task 5.7

Answer the following questions with respect to ratio analysis.

(a) An entity has an average gross profit margin of 23% and an average inventory turnover of 8 times, which is similar to the averages for the industry.

The entity is likely to be:

	✓
An architectural practice	
A supermarket	
An estate agent	
A manufacturer	

(b) Extracts from the financial statements of Taurus are as follows:

Statement of profit or loss	£000
Operating profit	230
Finance costs	(15)
Profit before tax	215
Income tax	(15)
Profit for the year	200

Statement of financial position	£000
Ordinary shares	2,000
Revaluation surplus	300
Retained earnings	1,200
	3,500
10% loan	1,000
Current liabilities	100
Total equity and liabilities	4,600

What is the return on capital employed?

	✓
5.1%	
4.7%	
6.6%	
6%	

(c) Managing the operating cycle is an important part of managing working capital in a company

Which of the following will increase the length of a company's operating cycle?

	✓
Reducing the receivables collection period	
Reducing the inventory holding period	
Reducing the payables payment period	
Reducing time taken to produce goods	

(d) Analysis of the financial statements of Capricorn at 31 December 20X8 yields the following information.

Gross profit margin	30%
Current ratio	2.14
ROCE	16.3%
Asset turnover	4.19
Inventory turnover	13.9

What is the operating profit margin?

	✓
3.9%	
7.6%	
16.1%	
7.1%	

Task 5.8

Forrest Limited is considering an acquisition of either Peas Limited or Carrots Ltd, which both operate in the same industry. You have been provided with extracts from the financial statements of both companies for the year ended 31 December 20X7.

Statements of profit and loss for the year ended 31 December 20X7

	Peas £000	Carrots £000
Revenue	12,000	20,500
Cost of sales	(10,500)	(18,000)
Gross profit	1,500	2,500
Operating expenses	(240)	(500)
Finance costs	(210)	(600)
Profit before tax	1,050	1,400
Income tax expense	(150)	(400)
Profit for the year	900	1,000
Note. Dividends paid during the year.	250	700

Statements of financial position as at 31 December 20X7

	Peas £000	Carrots £000
Non-current assets		
Freehold factory	2,600	Nil
Plant and machinery	5,000	7,400
	7,600	7,400
Current assets		
Inventory	2,000	3,600
Trade receivables	2,400	3,700
Bank	600	Nil
	5,000	7,300
Total assets	**12,600**	**14,700**
Equity and liabilities		
Equity shares of £1 each	2,000	2,000
Revaluation reserve	900	Nil
Retained earnings	2,600	800
	5,500	2,800
Non-current liabilities		
7% loan notes	3,000	3,200
10% loan notes	Nil	3,000
	3,000	6,200
Current liabilities		
Bank overdraft	Nil	1,700
Trade payables	3,100	3,800
Government grants	400	Nil
Taxation	600	200
	4,100	5,700
Total equity and liabilities	**12,600**	**14,700**

(a) **Calculate the following ratios for both companies, rounding off to ONE decimal place, or the nearest whole day:**

	Peas	Carrots
Return on year-end capital employed (ROCE)		
Gross profit margin		
Operating profit margin		
Current ratio		
Closing inventory holding period		
Trade receivables' collection period		
Trade payables' payment period		
Gearing		
Interest cover		
Dividend cover		

(b) **Critically appraise the relative performance and financial position of Peas and Carrots for the year ended 31 December 20X7, in light of the potential acquisition by Forrest.**

Profitability

Gearing

Liquidity

Summary

Task 5.9

The most recent financial statements of Tiger Tea plc (TTP) are shown below:

Statements of profit or loss for the year ended 31 December

	20X1 £000	20X0 £000
Revenue	25,500	17,250
Cost of sales	(14,800)	(10,350)
Gross profit	10,700	6,900
Distribution costs	(2,700)	(1,850)
Administrative expenses	(2,100)	(1,450)
Profit from operations	5,900	3,600
Finance costs	(650)	(100)
Profit before taxation	5,250	3,500
Income tax expense	(2,250)	(1,000)
Profit for the year	3,000	2,500

Statements of financial position as at 31 December

	20X1 £000	20X0 £000
ASSETS		
Non-current assets		
Property, plant and equipment	11,500	5,400
Intangibles	6,200	Nil
	17,700	5,400
Current assets		
Inventory	3,600	1,800
Trade receivables	2,400	1,400
Bank	Nil	4,000
	6,000	7,200
TOTAL ASSETS	**23,700**	**12,600**
EQUITY AND LIABILITIES		
Equity		
Equity shares of £1 each	5,000	5,000
Retained earnings	4,500	2,250
	9,500	7,250
Non-current liabilities		
5% loan notes	2,000	2,000
8% loan notes	7,000	Nil
	9,000	2,000
Current liabilities		
Bank overdraft	200	Nil
Trade payables	2,800	2,150
Current tax payable	2,200	1,200
	5,200	3,350
TOTAL EQUITY AND LIABILITIES	**23,700**	**12,600**

(a) Calculate the following ratios for each year, rounding off to ONE decimal place, or the nearest day.

	20X1	20X0
Net profit %		
Operating profit %		
Gross profit %		
ROCE		
ROE		
Gearing		
Interest cover		
Current ratio		
Quick ratio		

(b) Critically comment on the performance in 20X1 relative to 20X0 from the perspective of shareholders, under the following headings:

Profitability

Gearing

Liquidity

Chapter 6 – Internal controls: Accounting Systems and Controls/Financial Statements of Limited Companies/Management Accounting: Budgeting/Management Accounting: Decision and Control

Task 6.1

To date Rees Ltd has paid its suppliers by cheque. Rees Ltd now plans to pay larger suppliers by BACS, extending this method to all suppliers in time.

Complete the following statements.

Rees Ltd's plan is [▼] change.

Picklist:

a transformational
an incremental

The fact that the time of Rees Ltd's accounting staff will be freed up by not having to complete cheques by hand is [▼].

Picklist:

a tangible benefit of the change
a tangible cost of the change
an intangible benefit of the change
an intangible cost of the change

••

Task 6.2

You have been asked to identify some improvements to the controls in Sleeptight Ltd's sales ordering procedures.

- Sleeptight Ltd makes high-value bespoke wooden bedroom furniture to order.

- An official customer order is created for each sale by a sales executive. The order must state the product and agreed delivery date. It also states the approximate price.

- Customer orders must be reviewed and signed by the sales manager.

- Orders for more than three pieces of furniture for one customer must be signed by the sales director.

(a) **Identify ONE strength in these procedures. Explain how the business benefits from this.**

(b) **Identify ONE weakness in these procedures. Explain how this damages the business and suggest a remedy.**

(c) **Identify an opportunity to improve the procedures. Explain how the procedure should be changed and how the business could benefit.**

Task 6.3

You have been asked to suggest some improvements to the controls in Sleeptight Ltd's sales accounting procedures.

- Sleeptight Ltd makes high-value bespoke wooden bedroom furniture to order.

- The company operates an integrated accounting system which includes a sales accounting module. The sales manager is responsible for managing all sales activities.

- Before an order is taken from a new customer, the sales manager performs a credit check on them and obtains their banking details. The sales manager has the authority either to offer credit terms or to require payment by bank transfer before delivery of the furniture.

- Credit terms offered are always two months from the end of the month in which delivery takes place, with a 15% discount for payment within 10 days of delivery. Payment is required via bank transfer.

- All sales invoices are raised by the accounts receivable clerk, who produces the invoice by checking the despatch note to the customer order, then confirming the agreed price and terms with the sales manager.

- The accounts receivable clerk posts the invoices to the computerised accounting system, answers any queries from customers and issues credit notes when appropriate.

- The accounts receivable clerk checks the bank account weekly for bank transfers by customers and posts receipts to the ledger accounts.

(a) **Identify ONE strength in these procedures. Explain how the business benefits from this.**

(b) **Identify ONE weakness in these procedures. Explain how this damages the business and suggest a remedy.**

(c) **Identify an opportunity to improve the procedures. Explain how the procedure should be changed and how the business could benefit.**

Task 6.4

You have been asked to suggest some improvements to the controls in Sleeptight Ltd's purchase ordering procedures.

- Sleeptight Ltd makes high-value bespoke wooden bedroom furniture to order.

- All purchases, except petty cash items, must be documented on an official purchase order. The order should state the agreed price, if known.

- All departments are provided with books of pre-numbered order forms. These books can be obtained from the stationery store.

- Orders for production materials must be signed by the production manager.

- Capital expenditure orders must be signed by the finance director.

- There is no cash limit for purchase orders provided that they are within the approved budget.

- Other orders must be signed by the relevant budget holders.

- New suppliers are given a trade reference by the purchasing manager, who also requests credit terms. These are subject to negotiation, though the company's preferred terms are to pay 60 days from the end of the month in which delivery takes place.

(a) **Identify ONE strength in these procedures. Explain how the business benefits from this.**

(b) **Identify the weaknesses in these procedures. Explain how each one damages the business and suggest a remedy.**

(c) **Identify an opportunity to improve the procedures. Explain how the procedure should be changed and how the business could benefit.**

Task 6.5

You have been asked to suggest some improvements to the controls in Sleeptight Ltd's purchase accounting procedures.

- Sleeptight Ltd makes high-value bespoke wooden bedroom furniture to order.

- Four copies of each purchase order form are printed. Once signed, the original is sent to the supplier. A yellow copy is sent to the accounts payable clerk. A pink copy is retained by the individual who raised the order, while a green copy is sent to Goods Inwards.

- When the goods or service(s) are received, Goods Inwards checks the goods, signs the green copy and sends it to the accounts payable clerk.

- All purchase invoices received are checked by the accounts payable clerk, who checks the calculations, matches them to appropriate yellow and signed green copy orders and clears the invoices for payment.

- The accounts payable clerk posts the cleared invoices to the computerised accounting system and takes up queries with suppliers, requesting credit notes when appropriate.

- Invoices are automatically paid as they fall due through the bankers automated clearing system (BACS). The accounts payable clerk authorises one payment run every week.

- The accounts payable clerk is authorised to pay early if a discount of at least 5% is offered by the supplier.

(a) Identify the strengths in these procedures. Explain how the business benefits from these.

(b) Identify ONE weakness in these procedures. Explain how this damages the business and suggest a remedy.

Task 6.6

You have been asked to review the adequacy of the control in Sleeptight Ltd's payroll procedures.

The company operates an integrated accounting system which includes a payroll accounting module. The accounts manager, based at the head office, is responsible for managing payroll activities. The payroll clerk, based at the factory, performs day-to-day payroll tasks.

- Sleeptight Ltd makes high-value bespoke wooden bedroom furniture to order.

- Non-production staff are salaried and are not entitled to paid overtime.

- Production staff are all full-time. They are paid at time and a half their basic rate if they work more than 40 hours per week.

- Production staff sign themselves in and out of the factory each day, using the signing-in book which is kept in the staff locker room.

- Production staff record hours spent on individual items of bespoke furniture on job sheets that follow the items around the factory. These job sheets are checked and signed by production supervisors.

The payroll clerk:

- Maintains standing data on employees

- Calculates each employee's hours at work each week from the signing-in book

- Calculates gross pay and deductions for production staff weekly, and for other staff monthly

- Maintains the wages control account

- Prepares the bank payments each week/month to employees and HMRC

- Reconciles total pay and deductions in the wages control account

Once a month the accounts manager reviews total payroll cost against budget and investigates any large unexpected variances.

(a) **Identify ONE strength in these procedures. Explain how the business benefits from this.**

(b) **Identify the weaknesses in these procedures. Explain how these damage the business and suggest remedies.**

(c) **Identify an opportunity to improve the procedures. Explain how the procedure should be changed and how the business could benefit.**

Task 6.7

A company wishes to avoid or reduce certain specific risks in each of its three main transaction streams.

You are required to identify a control objective and control activity for each risk.

Transaction stream	Risk	Control objective	Control activity
Purchasing	Company pays for goods it does not receive		
Sales	Sales recorded late so fines incurred from HMRC with respect to VAT		
Payroll	Company overpays		

Task 6.8

You are presented with the monthly operating report below. The original budget has been flexed to the level of actual activity, and variances calculated.

You are told that:

- Material, labour and distribution costs are variable.
- Energy cost is semi-variable. The fixed element is budgeted at £12,800 per month.
- Equipment hire is a stepped cost, budgeted to increase at every 30,000 units of monthly production.
- Depreciation, marketing and administration costs are fixed.
- The company does not use full absorption costing.

Monthly operating report

Original budget		Flexed budget	Actual	Variance Fav/(Adv)
178,000	Sales volume (units)		192,000	
£		**£**	**£**	**£**
1,281,600	Sales revenue	1,382,400	1,377,000	−5,400
	Costs			
462,800	Materials	499,200	500,100	−900
480,600	Labour	518,400	516,500	1,900
67,640	Distribution	72,960	74,200	−1,240
60,860	Energy	64,640	65,080	−440
24,000	Equipment hire	28,000	28,600	−600
8,800	Depreciation	8,800	8,700	100
78,000	Marketing	78,000	78,900	−900
25,600	Administration	25,600	24,820	780
1,208,300	Total	1,295,600	1,296,900	−1,300
73,300	Operating profit/(loss)	86,800	80,100	−6,700

Write an email to the chief executive to explain the following.

(a) **The main factors that led to the actual profit being higher than the original budgeted profit.**

(b) **Whether improved internal controls might assist in controlling the adverse variances.**

Task 6.9

A company wishes to avoid or reduce certain specific risks in each of its three main transaction streams.

You are required to identify a control objective and control activity for each risk.

Transaction stream	Risk	Control objective	Control activity
Payroll	Company incurs fines from HMRC		
Sales	Custom lost through chasing payments already made by the customer		
Purchasing	Company pays the wrong supplier		

Task 6.10

A firm of accountants, Crachett & Co has decided to train all new staff in basic bookkeeping as part of their induction programme.

(a) **Identify the costs of such a decision, explaining the terms 'tangible costs' and 'intangible costs' in your response.**

As part of the reorganisation of the firm of accountants, other areas of the business are being reviewed. Crachett & Co are also considering a new accountancy software, however, it is expensive and the partners are unsure about whether to commit to it.

A software company, MoneyWise has quoted Crachett & Co for their new system.

Dear Sirs

Thank you for your interest in our fully integrated Client Pro Systems accounting system. We are happy to provide you with details of the following:

- Client Pro System 1 (Cloud).
- Sales ledger system, including pre-numbered invoices and aged debt reports.
- Purchases ledger system, incorporating purchase orders which can be matched against incoming invoices. Inventory aging reports are included.
- General ledger and summary trial balance reports.
- Exception reporting.
- Financial reporting tool for multi-client usage, incorporating iXBRL tax information, bookkeeping interface and payroll facility.
- Updates and upgrades occur regularly and will be automated at no extra cost.

Annual costs

	Initial costs	Annual costs
Client Pro system 1 (cloud)	£7,500 (to cover assistance with data migration)	£3,300 (up to 15 licensed users)

Training costs for the new system would be:

In-house training (maximum of 15 people)	£2,700
Course at local college (1 day)	£275 per person
Online course (completed in own time)	£75 per person (access limited to 6 months)

If you have any further questions, please do not hesitate to contact us.

Yours sincerely

E.Scrooge

Sales Director
MoneyWise

(b) **Evaluate the proposed new software, considering the factors in a cost-benefit analysis**

....

Answer Bank

Chapter 1 – The accounting function: Accounting Systems and Controls

Task 1.1

(a) If you want your accounting system to be integrated then you need to $\boxed{\text{centralise it}}$. A key benefit of integrating the company's accounting system is that you can ensure every area of the business complies with relevant $\boxed{\text{laws and regulations}}$.

(b)

Criterion	Centralised accounting function ✓	Decentralised accounting function ✓
More economies of scope	✓	
Better communication with business units		✓
Better placed to produce group accounts	✓	
More economies of scale	✓	

Task 1.2

Task	Responsible party
Preparation of budgetary control reports	Management accountant
Maintain accounting ledgers	Financial accountant
Cash management	Treasury manager

Task 1.3

Party	Responsibility
External auditors	Report whether the financial statements show a true and fair view
Accounting function	Maintain the accounting system
Directors	Prepare financial statements for the company

Task 1.4

(a)

	✓
Professional behaviour	
Objectivity	
Professional competence and due care	✓
Integrity	

(b)

Confidentiality
She must refuse to reveal the information and decline the trip

Task 1.5

(a)

Control activity	Type of security control
Passwords	Access control
Validation of input data	Integrity control
Archiving	System control

(b)

	✓
Mmmeee	
82s09PQ#	✓
1357abcd	

Task 1.6

	✓
Reverse the duplicate entries and advise the sales ledger team of his action	
Inform the sales invoicing team of the error	✓
Report the error to the chief accountant	
Prepare a credit note and send it to the customer	

Task 1.7

Error	Detected by reconciliation?
A batch of purchase invoices posted to the sales ledger control account	Yes
A pricing error in a sales invoice	No
VAT on a sales invoice posted to insurance rather than the VAT control account	No
A sales invoice posted to the wrong customer account	No
A sales invoice credited to the customer's account	Yes

Task 1.8

The proposed action violates the principle of segregation of duties. This means that different people should be responsible for different parts of the accounting system to minimise the chance of fraud and error.

For example, if Iqbal were to perform all of these functions he could potentially steal cash received from a customer and cover it up by writing off the debt or issuing a credit note.

If Iqbal were to make errors in performing his duties, for example issuing the same invoice twice (as in Task 1.6), then the chances of it being detected are reduced if there are no other people involved. It is much easier to spot errors made by other people than to spot your own.

Finally, Iqbal could well become overburdened by his increased responsibilities. This is likely to lead to more errors and also a lack of efficiency in, for example, chasing customers for payment.

Task 1.9

Iqbal has breached the principle of confidentiality. He has gained information during the course of his employment and should not reveal that information to any unauthorised person, without the prior consent of all parties; nor should he use it for his own purposes.

Iqbal should not reveal the information to a third party and he should also not reveal the information to anyone within JSL who does not require the information by virtue of their duties. For example, it would be acceptable to reveal the information to the Chief Accountant but not to the payroll clerk.

Iqbal may also be considered to have breached the principle of professional behaviour, by spreading rumours about TL Ltd. Iqbal has no confirmed evidence that TL is, in fact, in financial difficulty.

Task 1.10

	✓
A discussion of sales figures for the main three products of JSL	
Highlighting the employee volunteering opportunities from a team helping to re-turf a school football pitch	✓
Reporting on the recycling efforts within the office environment	✓
Reporting any incidents of money laundering and how the organisation seeks to change its controls going forward	✓

A sustainability report will look at any non-compliance with regulations (money laundering), any organisational efforts to reduce the environmental impact (recycling) and raising awareness of social responsibility (helping out a local school). The sales figures are more likely to be mentioned as part of performance within a director's report (if at all) to support any going concern worries by stakeholders, or more likely, to not be mentioned in any great detail in public financial statements.

Chapter 2 – Budgetary reporting: Accounting Systems and Controls/Management Accounting: Budgeting/Management Accounting: Decision and Control

Task 2.1

(a) Performance indicators

A number of assumptions have been made in this budget and we need to monitor their achievement.

Raw material costs are variable and we should expect them to increase or decrease with production levels. I recommend that we review the following four indicators on a weekly basis.

- Material usage per unit of production
- Percentage of material wastage
- Price per kilogram
- Number of days of inventory held

Variations in any of these indicators will impact on overall materials cost, and so should be monitored closely.

(b) Forecasts

Although the production manager should take ownership of this budget there are aspects of it which are not wholly within his control.

- Purchase prices will be negotiated by the purchasing manager. The two managers need to work together to balance quality with price.

- Wastage is an important factor and is at least partly dependent upon quality. The wastage level has been estimated for budget purposes and must be monitored carefully.

- A reduction in inventory is planned. This will only be sensible if the supplier proves to be more reliable, as anticipated.

- Finally, the production manager cannot control production demand, although allowance for this can be made with budget flexing.

(c) Lack of goal congruence

The purchasing manager's performance will be assessed on his ability to acquire raw materials for the lowest possible unit cost and the production manager will be assessed on his ability to manage the production of finished goods at the lowest possible cost. This could lead to conflicts due to a lack of goal congruence in two main areas.

(i) Material usage:

The production manager will aim to use the least amount of raw materials to achieve budgeted production. However the purchasing manager is likely to be able to negotiate a lower price per kilogram if more kilograms are purchased.

(ii) Cost and quality:

The purchasing manager will want to acquire raw materials for the lowest possible cost, yet low cost materials might be of poor quality, which will impact on wastage levels and therefore materials usage. This will have adverse consequences for the production manager.

Task 2.2

(a)

Operating budget	Scenario A	Scenario B
Sales price (£ per unit)	6.00	6.30
Sales volume (units)	84,000	75,600
	£	£
Sales revenue	504,000	476,280
Costs		
Material	201,600	181,440
Labour	226,800	204,120
Energy	17,680	18,020
Depreciation	8,100	7,200
Total	454,180	410,780
Gross profit	49,820	65,500
Increase/(decrease) in gross profit		15,680

Workings

Sales price = £6.00 × 1.05 = £6.30

Sales volume = 84,000 × 90% = 75,600 units

Sales revenue = 75,600 × £6.30 = £476,280

Materials = £201,600 × 90% = £181,440

Labour = £226,800 × 90% = £204,120

Energy = £17,680 × 1.06/1.04 = £18,020

Depreciation = £8,100 × 8/9 = £7,200

(b) **Financial factors**

The benefits of centralising the administrative and financial parts of the SWP business would result in efficiencies in terms of avoiding duplication of roles (a centrally based payroll team, rather than multiple teams in the local sites).

The potential drawbacks would involve short term higher costs due to potential redundancies of staff, relocation expenditure for retained staff, training costs to ensure consistencies of approach and capital expenditure to ensure the head office can house the increased staff with the necessary equipment.

Control environment

By having a central team working on financial and administration tasks, all of the tasks are being completed by one team, which is easier and more controllable. The controls surrounding the completion of the financial records can be more closely monitored by management due to the proximity of the teams.

Month end and annual accounting processes should be more efficient, as different teams of accounts payable, accounts receivable, treasury etc can work together as they are in the same location.

There can be standardised and consistent procedures which are more easily controlled if the staff are in the same location. Different approaches or timescales are avoided.

More specialised knowledge can be held in one location, for example, human resources and payroll can be centralised on one site, allowing close working and timely interactions between the different disciplines.

However, the interim period once any announcement has been made to the company may result in low productivity of staff (the threat of redundancy or fear of the unknown), low morale and potentially poor levels of control especially from the local sites.

Decision-making factors

Decisions can be made taking into account the whole company view, rather than relying on the potentially differing opinions of the site teams, which should lead to increased goal congruence.

Major decisions, such as capital expenditure, recruitment and training can be centrally debated and decided upon, making the process more efficient and arguably better informed as the results from all sites can be considered.

However, it is possible that analysis and decision making would become more remote from the operational centres, and a reduced direct involvement with the manufacturing sites of the company.

In the long term view, centralising the financial and administrative knowledge and operations makes financial sense resulting in improved controls and decision making efficiency. However, it is likely that SPW would have some short term financial impacts to absorb as well as working with a work force who may have low morale at work.

Task 2.3

Monthly operating report

Original budget		Flexed budget	Actual	Variance Fav/(Adv)
178,000	Sales volume (units)		192,000	
£		£	£	£
1,281,600	Sales revenue	1,382,400	1,377,000	−5,400
	Costs			
462,800	Materials	499,200	500,100	−900
480,600	Labour	518,400	516,500	1,900
67,640	Distribution	72,960	74,200	−1,240
60,860	Energy	64,640	65,080	−440
24,000	Equipment hire	28,000	28,600	−600
8,800	Depreciation	8,800	8,700	100
78,000	Marketing	78,000	78,900	−900
25,600	Administration	25,600	24,820	780
1,208,300	Total	1,295,600	1,296,900	−1,300
73,300	Operating profit/(loss)	86,800	80,100	−6,700

Workings

Flexed sales revenue = £1,281,600 × $\dfrac{192,000}{178,000}$ = £1,382,400

Energy original budget = £12,800 fixed, so £48,060 variable

Flexed energy cost = £12,800 + $\left(£48,060 \times \dfrac{192}{178} \right)$ = £64,640

Flexed equipment hire = £24,000 × $\dfrac{7}{6}$ = £28,000

Task 2.4

(a) Reasons for variances

I have reviewed the results for the period. There was an operating profit of £198,000 compared with the flexed budget profit of £196,000. The original budget anticipated a profit of £227,000 based on higher sales of 165,000 units.

Compared with the original budget, the result is disappointing and this is attributed to a loss of sales volume due to price competition. The volume was 11% below the original budget despite our own 10% price reduction during the year. The flexed budget calculations indicate that lost sales should have generated a profit of £31,000 (£227,000 less £196,000). The flexed budget is based on the original but with appropriate volume adjustments.

The unforeseen competition has taken sales volume from us and forced us to make 10% price reductions. The full year impact of the price reduction is significant and we are not confident that volume will recover fully. This situation might have been avoided with better market intelligence and a proactive marketing campaign.

Compared with the flexed budget there was an adverse sales variance of £29,000 (3.8%), caused by the 10% price reduction part way through the year.

However, there was a £9,000 favourable variance on material costs (4%) where both material price and usage were lower than budgeted. Similarly, the labour cost variance was £15,000 favourable (12%). With production volumes less than budgeted there was less need to work overtime at premium rate plus better quality materials resulted in improved efficiencies and less waste requiring rework.

(b) Setting and managing the budget

To be challenging, budgets should be stretching, always striving for improvement, whilst being achievable. We can see from the operating statement that the adverse sales variance was counterbalanced by unrelated and fortuitous favourable cost variances in materials and labour. It can be argued that the budget was poorly focused, failing to address the threat of competition and not challenging managers to improve efficiency.

I recommend that we introduce closer scrutiny at the budget setting stage to ensure that budgetary slack is not permitted and that efficiency improvements are planned and introduced. A stretching budget is likely to motivate managers to improve performance. Variances need to be fully analysed and explained on a regular basis and corrective action taken promptly.

(c)   Standard costing

> Standard costing is an effective mechanism for bringing rigour to budgetary control. It makes sense to set standards for production resources at the level of a single unit of production. The standards can be multiplied by planned production levels to create cost budgets.
>
> The system facilitates the calculation of detailed cost variances which helps managers to understand and manage the resources effectively. Looking at the operating statement, for example, we could analyse the material variance into the price and efficiency aspects and also see whether the labour variance was wholly due to saved overtime premium.

Task 2.5

Impact on profit of increasing fixed costs but reducing variable costs

> For each unit sold, selling price minus variable costs is termed as 'contribution'; each unit sold contributes a certain amount towards covering the fixed costs of the business. When the total contribution (from all units sold) exactly matches fixed costs then the business makes a profit of zero. This is termed the break-even point. When total contribution exceeds fixed costs, the amount of the excess is profit.
>
> If fixed costs increase, this will mean that more total contribution will need to be generated in order to cover the fixed costs. However the reduction in variable costs means that each unit generates more contribution per unit. Whether the increased contribution per unit is an advantage relative to the increased fixed costs depends on the number of units expected to be sold.
>
> The ratio of incremental fixed costs/incremental variable cost per unit can be used to establish the number of units at which we are economically indifferent. If, for example, increased fixed costs of £10,000 are balanced by a decrease of £2 per unit, then £10,000/2 = 5,000. This tells us that if sales are likely to be below 5,000 units we would make more profit by not making the change, as the increase in fixed costs exceeds the increased contribution. If sales are likely to be above 5,000 units the increased contribution exceeds the increased fixed costs. At exactly 5,000 units the increase in fixed costs is the same as the decrease in total variable costs, and so we are indifferent.

Task 2.6

Limiting factors

> The usual decision rule is that we should make and sell the maximum possible of the products which generate the highest amount of contribution per unit, so as to maximise total contribution and thereby profit.
>
> When any factors of production are in short supply, we term these as 'limiting factors' in that they limit our ability to produce as much as we would like of our products which require this limited resource.
>
> The decision rule then changes, so that we should maximise the contribution per unit of limiting factor. We calculate this by dividing contribution per unit by the quantity per unit of the limiting factor required. We should rank the three products which use this factor and produce the highest ranked product until we reach the limit of its demand. We should then do the same with the product ranked second, then third, until we have exhausted the amount of the product in short supply.
>
> This, unlike a 20% cut across the board, focusses production on the productions which generate the most contribution per unit of limiting factor and thereby maximise profit. It should also be noted that, since only three products require this material, there is no need to reduce production across other products.

Task 2.7

Pricing of special order

> Total cost per unit includes variable cost plus the amount of fixed costs which have been absorbed into the unit, according to the business's overhead absorption method. Sales price must normally be set higher than total cost, in order to ensure that all costs, both fixed and variable, are covered.
>
> In this particular case, the special order would be in addition to the business's normal production. Presumably the price of the normal production has been set to ensure that all costs, including the fixed costs, have been covered by the sale of the normal level of production. This means that the price on the special order only needs to be higher than the additional variable costs, as fixed costs have already been covered by normal production. Any sales price in excess of £187 will generate additional profit for the business.
>
> At the same time, setting the price this low may not be a wise idea. If any existing customers discover that a new customer is being charged less than the normal price of £400 they are likely to be unhappy and may take their business elsewhere. If the one-off order becomes a regular order, it would be difficult for us to increase the price to a more sustainable level later.

Chapter 3 – Accounting control systems and procedures: Accounting Systems and Controls

Task 3.1

Allocating a payment from one customer to another customer's account in order to balance the books and detract from a shortfall is called | teeming and lading | .

Task 3.2

	✓
False representation	✓
Failure to segregate duties	
Failure to disclose information	✓
Abuse of position	✓
Duress and undue influence	

Task 3.3

Systemic weakness	Understatement of reported profit ✓	Overstatement of reported profit ✓
Overvaluation of inventory at the period end		✓
Creating an unnecessary allowance for doubtful debts	✓	
Fictitious sales		✓
Not writing off irrecoverable debts		✓
Overstating expenses	✓	

Task 3.4

Systemic weakness	Misappropriation of assets ✓	Misstatement in the financial statements ✓
Leaving offices where computers are held unlocked	✓	
Failing to maintain an asset register		✓
Omitting inventory from the annual physical count		✓
Creating a fictitious employee on the payroll	✓	✓
Failing to chase unpaid debts		✓

Task 3.5

Segregation of duties is a type of | staff control | over fraud in the accounting system.

Task 3.6

No.	Weakness	Potential problem
1	The sales manager appears to have very little involvement in day to day sales, apart from negotiating terms with new customers.	Failures in the system and system abuses could go unnoticed.
2	The procedures do not include any mention of quality control checks ensuring that goods of the correct category and standard have been despatched.	If this is not happening the company could be sending out sub-standard goods.
3	Orders can be taken without agreeing a price.	The company is in a weak position to negotiate price after the goods have been despatched.

No.	Weakness	Potential problem
4	Despatch signs the green copy of the order, but there is no signed goods received note from the customer, confirming receipt of the goods.	Goods could be delivered to the wrong address, or no delivered at all and still charged for. This could cause problems with customer goodwill as well as creating potential for fraud.
5	Lack of authorisation of new accounts.	There should be a policy for deciding on whether to offer any credit at all. Potential for fraud through collusion with customers.
6	The terms agreed by the sales manager are not countersigned.	Potential for fraud through collusion with customers.
7	Only one signature is required on most orders.	Potential for fraud through collusion with customers.
8	The accounts receivable clerk checks, clears and arranges payment of invoices. She also handles customer queries, issues credit notes and records the receipt of payments. There is a lack of segregation of duties.	Potential for fraud through collusion with customers.
8	The sales manager and accounts receivable clerk control all aspects of sales accounting.	Potential for fraud through collusion.
9	Cash receipts are only monitored and posted once a week.	Increases the opportunity for teeming and lading, and means a bad service will be given to customers if they ring with a query.
10	No counter-signatory required for credit notes.	Potential for fraud through collusion with customers.

Task 3.7

	✓
Physical controls	
Segregation of duties	✓
Management controls	
Supervisory controls	✓
Organisation	
Authorisation (approval) of transactions	✓
Arithmetic and bookkeeping checks	
Personnel controls	

Task 3.8

Note. Other valid weaknesses may have been identified and would gain credit.

No.	Weakness	Potential problem
1	Only hand-written notes are made rather than a pre-numbered requisition form.	Requisition details might be lost and might not be followed up. As they are hand written, it could be difficult to read the writing and errors could be made.
2	Requisitions are not authorised.	Employees could order goods for their own use or that the business does not need.
3	Purchasing manager should obtain quotations from several suppliers.	The company could pay higher prices than necessary, hence wasting resources.
4	There is no system for recording receipt of other goods and services.	The company may pay for other goods and services which have not been received.

No.	Weakness	Potential problem
5	Invoices are only matched to purchase orders 'if they are available'. There is no mention of investigating missing purchase orders. No goods should be ordered without a valid purchase order.	The company could receive goods which have not been ordered, or are not authorised.
6	Purchases ledger clerk performs too many tasks.	There is increased chance of fraud or error.
7	Invoices are not authorised before being paid.	There is increased risk of fraud or error.

Task 3.9

Note. Other valid weaknesses may have been identified and would gain credit.

No.	Weakness	Potential problem
1	Blank timekeeping cards are used. These should be pre-printed with the employee name and number and should be pre-numbered.	Timekeeping cards could go missing.
2	There is no supervision over the signing in or signing out and no ID is required.	Employees could record fictitious hours and employees could sign in or out for their colleagues.
3	No independent personnel function.	Supervisors and wages clerk could add fictitious employees to the payroll and misappropriate their wages.
4	Lack of segregation of duties with the wages clerk.	The wages clerk could misappropriate funds.
5	No control over weekly payroll, such as reconciling it to the prior month's payroll.	Hours worked could be incorrectly entered.
6	Only one person banks the cheque, collects the cash and draws up the pay packets.	Cash cheque could be misappropriated either before reaching wages clerk or by the wages clerk.

No.	Weakness	Potential problem
7	The pay packets are not checked against the payroll and signed for by the supervisors when they take control of them.	Pay packets could be incorrect or could go missing, resulting in a loss of cash to the company (if the packets are too high) or disgruntled staff (if the packets are too low or if they are missing).
8	Employees do not count and sign for their pay packets and their IDs are not required.	Employees could claim not to have been paid, or could dispute the amount of their pay packets raising unpleasant disputes with the company, which could result in financial losses to the company.
9	Inadequate control over the distribution itself. There is only one supervisor present and it is not a formal process.	Supervisors could sign for absent or terminated employees and collect their wages.
10	No procedure for unclaimed wages.	Unclaimed wages could be misappropriated.
11	Poor control over hiring employees: job vacancies are not authorised, there is no mention of an interviewing process and no mention of authorising the employment contract.	Staff could be hired without the necessary references and qualifications. Unnecessary staff could be hired, who are not needed and fictitious staff could be created and their pay misappropriated.
12	Verbal authorisation for pay increases.	Increases could be made that are not authorised, resulting in the misappropriation of funds, or resulting in a payroll that the company cannot afford.

Chapter 4 – Decision making and control: Accounting Systems and Controls/Management Accounting: Decision and Control

Task 4.1

The ┃ fixed overheads ┃ total variance may be analysed into expenditure, efficiency and capacity variances.

Task 4.2

Complete the following statements:

(a) The standard quantity of labour per unit is ┃ 15 ┃ minutes.

(b) The standard quantity of materials needed to produce 13,500 units of X07 is ┃ 16,875 ┃ litres.

(c) The standard labour hours to produce 12,000 units of X07 is ┃ 3,000 ┃ hours.

(d) The standard labour cost to produce 13,500 units of X07 is ┃ £ ┃ 57,375 ┃.

(e) The standard overhead absorption rate per unit is ┃ £ ┃ 5.50 ┃.

Workings

(a) 3,500 direct labour hours/14,000 units = 0.25 hours (15 minutes)

(b) Standard quantity per unit = 17,500 litres/14,000 units = 1.25 litres

13,500 units × 1.25 litres = 16,875 litres

(c) Standard labour hours per unit = 0.25 hours (see part (a))

12,000 units × 0.25 hours = 3,000 hours

(d) Standard labour cost per unit = £59,500/14,000 units = £4.25

13,500 units × £4.25 hours = £57,375

(e) Standard OAR = £77,000/14,000 units = £5.50 per unit

Task 4.3

(a) The standard cost per kilogram is ┃ £ ┃ 2.50 ┃.

Working

£10,915 – £1,665 = £9,250 standard cost

Standard cost per kilogram = £9,250/3,700 kilograms = £2.50

(b) The material usage variance is £ 6,000 | Adverse .

Working

19,000 units should use (× 10 litres per unit)	190,000 litres
But did use	200,000 litres
Material usage variance in litres	10,000 litres (A)
× standard cost per litre (£132,000/220,000 litres)	× £0.60
Material usage variance in £	£6,000 (A)

(c) The total labour efficiency variance is £ 4,500 | Favourable .

The idle time variance is £ 6,000 | Adverse .

Working

Labour efficiency variance

12,000 units should have taken (× 0.6 hours)	7,200 hrs
But did take	6,900 hrs
	300 hrs (F)
At standard rate	× £15.00
Efficiency variance	£4,500 (F)

Idle time variance

7,300 hours – 6,900 hours = 400 hours idle time

400 hours × £15.00 = £6,000 (A)

Task 4.4

The fixed overhead volume variance is £ 25,000 | Favourable .

Working

	£
OAR is £350,000/28,000 = £12.50 per unit	
Actual production @ standard OAR 30,000 × £12.50	375,000
Budgeted production @ standard OAR 28,000 × £12.50	350,000
Volume variance	25,000 (F)

The actual fixed production overheads incurred were £ 315,000 .

Working

	£
Budgeted overhead	350,000
Actual overhead (Balancing figure)	315,000
Expenditure variance	35,000 (F)

Task 4.5

Variance	Amount £	Adverse/ Favourable
Fixed overhead capacity	448,000	Favourable
Fixed overhead efficiency	268,000	Adverse

Workings

Fixed overhead capacity variance

	£
OAR is £3,840,000/480,000 = £8.00 per labour hour	
Actual hours @ standard OAR 536,000 × £8.00	4,288,000
Budgeted hours @ standard OAR 480,000 × £8.00	3,840,000
Capacity variance	448,000 (F)

Fixed overhead efficiency variance

	£
Standard hours for actual production @ standard OAR 67,000 × 7.5 hours × £8.00	4,020,000
Actual hours @ standard OAR 536,000 × £8.00	4,288,000
Efficiency variance	268,000 (A)

Task 4.6

			£
Budgeted variable cost for actual production			387,600
Budgeted fixed cost			234,000
Total budgeted cost for actual production			621,600
Variance	**Favourable £**	**Adverse £**	
Direct materials price	18,700		
Direct materials usage	11,900		
Direct labour rate		28,560	
Direct labour efficiency		12,240	
Fixed overhead expenditure	13,000		
Fixed overhead volume	N/A	N/A	
Total variance	43,600	40,800	−2,800
Actual cost of actual production			618,800

Workings

Budgeted variable cost per unit = (£130,200 + £223,200)/12,400 units = £28.50

Budgeted variable cost for actual production = 13,600 units × £28.50 = £387,600

Total budgeted cost for actual production = £387,600 + £234,000 (fixed costs)

= £621,600

Direct labour efficiency variance

13,600 units should have taken (× 2 hours)	27,200 hrs
But did take	28,560 hrs
	1,360 hrs (A)
At standard rate	× £9.00
Efficiency variance	£12,240 (A)

Fixed overhead expenditure variance = Actual £13,000 lower than budgeted, so favourable.

Task 4.7

(a) The part of the variance explained by the increase in the price index is

£ | 281,250 (A) .

Working

	£
12,500 litres × £450 (original standard rate)	5,625,000
12,500 litres × £472.50 (£450 × 126.525/120.50)	5,906,250
	281,250 (A)

(b) The part of the variance not explained by the increase in the price index is

£ 93,750 .

Working

£375,000 – £281,250 = £93,750

(c) The percentage increase in the index is [5] %.

Working

(126.525 – 120.50)/120.50 = 0.05 (5%)

(d)

	September 20X3 £	December 20X3 £
Cost per kilogram of Z4QX	2,136.62	2,543.84

Workings

Difference between April 20X3 and May 20X3 = £135.74

Difference between May 20X3 and June 20X3 = £135.74

September 20X3 cost = £1,729.40 (June 20X3) + (£135.74 × 3) = £2,136.62

December 20X3 cost = £2,136.62 (September X3) + (£135.74 × 3) = £2,543.84

(e) The forecast cost per kilogram, using the regression line, for September 20X3 is £ 118.85 .

Workings

June 20X3 is period 41. Therefore September 20X3 = period 44.

$y = 24.69 + 2.14x$ where y = cost per kilogram   x = the period

$y = 24.69 + (2.14 × 44)$

$y = £118.85$

Task 4.8

Total direct material variance

The total direct material variance simply compares the **flexed budget** for materials with the actual cost incurred. The flexed budget is the total budgeted cost of materials for the actual production; 21,000 units in this example. It is incorrect to calculate the variance as £74,500 adverse by comparing the actual cost of £954,500 with the original budgeted cost of £880,000.

The flexing of the budget calculates the **quantity of materials** which are expected to be used to produce the **actual production**. Therefore, the expected usage of materials to produce 21,000 units is £924,000 (if 80,000 kilograms costing £880,000 is required to make 20,000 units then it follows, assuming that the material cost and quantity is perfectly variable, that to make 21,000 units requires 84,000 kilograms at a cost of £11 per kilogram (£880,000/80,000)).

This flexed budget can now be **compared with the actual** costs to produce the total material variance of £30,500. This variance is adverse because the **actual cost was greater than the flexed budgeted cost**.

This total variance can now be split into two elements:

- The variance due to the price being different to that which was expected: the material price variance.
- The variance due to the quantity of material used per unit of production being different to that which was expected: the material usage variance.

The expected (standard or budgeted or planned) price is £11 per kilogram (£880,000/80,000) and therefore the expected cost of 83,000 kilograms must be 83,000 kilograms at £11 per kilogram. This is £913,000.

The price variance can now be calculated by taking the actual cost (price paid) for the 83,000 kilograms and comparing this to the expected cost. This results in £913,000, compared to £954,500: a variance of £41,500. This variance is adverse because the **actual cost is greater than the expected cost**.

The material usage variance is calculated by taking the quantity of materials which would be expected to be used to produce the actual volume of production. In this case 21,000 units were produced and the expected quantity of materials for each unit is 4 kilograms (80,000 kilograms/20,000 units). Therefore, to produce 21,000 units requires 84,000 kilograms of material. Compare this to the actual quantity used of 83,000 kilograms produces a variance of 1,000 kilograms. This is favourable and needs to be **valued at the expected cost** of £11 per kilogram, giving £11,000.

The usage variance is always **valued at the standard cost** (expected/planned or budgeted) because the price variance has already been isolated. If both variances have been calculated correctly they should reconcile back to the total materials variance. In this example, the price variance of £41,500 adverse less the £11,000 favourable usage variance is reconciled to the total variance of £30,500 adverse.

Task 4.9

(a)

	Scenario 1	Scenario 2
Return on capital employed	11.96%	9.52%
Inventory holding period in days	50.00	45.29
Sales price per unit	£14.00	£12.00
Full production cost per unit	£9.00	£9.00

Workings

Return on capital employed
Scenario 1 = £275,000/£2,298,400 × 100% = 11.96%
Scenario 2 = £200,000/£2,100,340 × 100% = 9.52%

Inventory holding period
Scenario 1 = £147,950/(£1,680,000 – £600,000) × 365 = 50.00 days
Scenario 2 = £167,500/(£1,800,000 – £450,000) × 365 = 45.29 days

Sales price per unit
Scenario 1 = £1,680,000/120,000 = £14.00
Scenario 2 = £1,800,000/150,000 = £12.00

Full production cost per unit
Scenario 1 = (£1,680,000 – £600,000)/120,000 = £9.00
Scenario 2 = (£1,800,000 – £450,000)/150,000 = £9.00

(b)

	Scenario 3
Capital employed (£)	175,000
Return on capital employed (%)	13
Profit margin (%)	14
Gearing (%)	32.75
Profit (to the nearest £)	22,750
Sales revenue (to the nearest £)	162,500

Workings

Profit (to the nearest £) = £175,000 × (13/100) = £22,750

Sales revenue (to the nearest £) = £22,750 ÷ (14/100) = £162,500

(c)

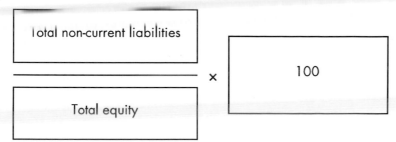

Or

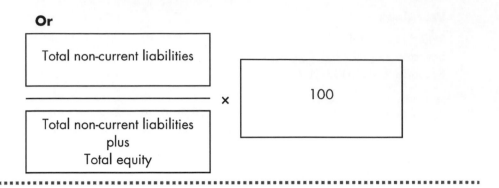

$$\frac{\text{Total non-current liabilities}}{\begin{array}{c}\text{Total non-current liabilities}\\ \text{plus}\\ \text{Total equity}\end{array}} \times \boxed{100}$$

....

Task 4.10

(a)

	Product Tig £	Product Tag £
The contribution per unit is	1,200	1,350
The contribution per kilogram of materials is	200	180

Workings

Contribution per unit

Product Tig = £4,000 – £2,800 = £1,200
Product Tag = £4,950 – £3,600 = £1,350

Contribution per kilogram of material

Product Tig = £1,200/6 kg = £200
Product Tag = £1,350/7.5 kg = £180

(b) The optimal production order for products Tig and Tag is $\boxed{\text{Tig then Tag}}$.

(Based on the contribution per kilogram of material calculated in part (a)).

(c)

	Product Tig	Product Tag
Production in units	200	240

Workings

Supply is limited to 3,000 kilograms of material

Product Tig then Tag (based on part (b))

200 units of Tig × 6 kg per unit = 1,200 kg (so 1,800 kg remaining to produce Tag)

1,800 kg/7.5 kg per unit = 240 units of Tag

(d)

	Product Tig £	Product Tag £
Total contribution	240,000	324,000

Workings

Product Tig = 200 units × £1,200 = £240,000
Product Tag = 240 units × £1,350 = £324,000

(e)

Should Alpha Ltd purchase the additional material?	Give a reason
(1) Yes	**(2)** The additional cost per kilogram is less than the contribution per kilogram.

Task 4.11

(a)

	Sales price £40	Sales price £50
The target total production cost per unit	£28	£35
The target fixed production cost per unit	£16	£22
The target total fixed production cost	£8,000,000	£9,460,000

Workings

Target total production cost per unit
Sales price £40 = £40 × 70/100 = £28
Sales price £50 = £50 × 70/100 = £35

Target fixed production cost per unit
Sales price £40 = £28 − £12 = £16
Sales price £50 = £35 − £13 = £22

Target fixed production cost
Sales price £40 = £16 per unit × 500,000 = £8,000,000
Sales price £50 = £22 per unit × 430,000 = £9,460,000

(b) Alpha should set the price at [£50] in order to achieve the target profit margin.

....

Task 4.12

To: Finance director **Subject:** Variances
From: Accounting technician **Date:** Today

(a) Sales volume

> The sales volume is expected to double.
>
> The volume increase will increase the profit margin if the fixed costs remain constant.
>
> In this case the fixed production costs are remaining unchanged and therefore the increased volume will improve the gross profit margin (GPM).

Materials cost

> The material cost per unit reduces by 20% to £4 per unit which will also improve the margin for the proposed position. The doubling of the volume is likely to allow the company to purchase in greater quantities and access additional discounts.

Labour cost

> The labour cost per unit is unchanged and therefore has no effect on the margin.
>
> There have been no economies of scale or learning effect.

Fixed production costs

> The fixed production costs are constant in total but the important point is that they are spread over more units. The proposed position increases the volume by 2x (200%) which reduces the fixed cost per unit. Fixed costs per unit reduce by 50%. This will improve the margin for the proposed position.

(b) Inventory levels

> Inventory levels are likely to increase significantly because the volume of demand is expected to be higher and therefore higher inventory levels will be needed to fulfil orders. Based upon the current inventory levels in relation to turnover the forecast position will be that inventory levels may increase to around £560,000 (current inventory days = 350,000/ 2,250,000 × 365 = 56.78 days, therefore inventory will become (£3.6 million/365) × 56.78 days = £560,000).

Trade receivable levels

> Trade receivables' levels are likely to increase significantly because the turnover increases. The current position is that trade receivable days are 55.3 days (500/3,300) × 365. Therefore assuming similar profile trade receivables will increase to around £820k (5,400,000/365) × 55.3 = £818k.

Task 4.13

(a) Credit controller

> Currently the assessment of creditworthiness, setting of credit limits, and chasing of debts is performed by sales staff. Sales staff may not have experience in credit control and may, while acting entirely with good intentions, extend credit to a customer who is not credit worthy. They could be tempted to give credit to customers without thoroughly checking their financial situation. Sales staff should not be responsible for chasing overdue receivables, as they may be reluctant to push hard for payment for fear of damaging the relationship with customers. They are also likely to see the task as low priority and prefer to spend their time generating sales and thereby gaining commission.
>
> The new credit controller should perform a thorough assessment of new customers before setting a credit limit, which should be authorised by the sales manager. The credit controller should chase payment of overdue receivables, which should happen before they are 120 days overdue.

BPP
LEARNING MEDIA

Sales manager

Sales staff have freedom to set sales discounts, and may set unrealistic discounts to achieve their sales targets. SSSL then loses out on potential revenue. Sales staff are also able to access the customer master file to enter discounts, which could result in fraud or error.

The sales manager should set out clear policies for the award of discounts and then authorise any discounts given. The sales manager should then update the master files. The sales manager should also introduce procedures to improve the documentation in the sales system, such as having sequentially numbered sales orders rather than an email to the accounting and despatch departments. As stated above, the sales manager should also authorise credit limits.

(b) Cost implications

SSSL will have additional payroll costs to bear. The credit controller's salary will be a fixed cost but the sales manager's salary is likely to be semi-variable, as the role is likely to carry some sales-related remuneration. These costs will increase the break-even point and impact on profit, although hopefully the involvement of the sales manager will increase sales and that of the credit controller will reduce bad debt expenses.

Resentment of sales staff

The filling of these two roles could cause resentment among sales staff. They will lose a lot of their freedom to operate autonomously , may interpret the appointments as being criticism of their abilities, and could be obstructive. They could leave SSSL, leaving the company with a shortage of experienced staff.

Task 4.14

If Roe were to stop being produced, the company would lose the benefit of the contribution generated by Roe, but would save on the fixed costs:

	£
Loss of contribution	(30,000)
Savings in fixed costs	10,000
Incremental loss	(20,000)

If production stopped on Roe, the company would see a fall of £20,000 in their profits.

The profit generated by Codlings would be as follows:

	£
Contribution	24,000
Directly attributable fixed costs	(12,000)
Incremental profit	12,000

If production was switched to Codlings, Gritby would only make £12,000 profit, so the company would suffer an overall drop in profits of £8,000.

They should, therefore, keep making Roe in preference to Codlings.

Task 4.15

(a)

	Blossom £000	
Revenue (2,850 × 1.4)	3,990.0	
Materials (784 × 1.4 × 0.95)	1,042.7	
Direct labour (448 × 1.4)	627.2	
Fixed production overheads (420 + 100)	520.0	
Cost of sales	2,189.9	
Gross profit	1,800.1	45.1%
Sales and distribution costs (640 × 1.4)	896.0	
Administration costs (250 + 60)	310.0	
Profit from operations	594.1	14.9%

(b)

Dandelion should be closed down if the decision was based solely on the financial data.

(1) This is because the company will be more profitable;
(2) Current profit = £150,000 + £308,000 = £458,000
(3) New profit = £594,100

(c)   Any one of the following suggested answers.

- **Staff morale** – staff will either need to be redeployed or made redundant, which negatively impacts morale and motivation.

- **Customers** – as the product made and sold by Dandelion is different from that of Blossom and the local retailers do not buy from both subsidiaries, it is possible that Daisy could adversely impact the success of these local retailers. The Dandelion range sources from local materials, which is unique selling point. By ceasing this range, Daisy could adversely impact their company image, and potentially even impact the Blossom range's appeal.

- **Suppliers** – some suppliers may be reliant on the organisation to stay in business. If the organisation chooses to stop making the product this could have severe consequences on these local suppliers, especially the local wood supplier.

Task 4.16

(a)

The loss of a proportion of financial and customer staff will likely have affected staff morale amongst the remaining staff in these departments. This could have affected their commitment to the company and been detrimental to the customer experience. Less staff could also have affected accuracy and there could potentially be errors in the accounts.

- The reduction in staff is likely to explain some of the reduction of £774,000 in administrative expenses (financial staff) and increase in distribution costs (of £1,010,000) due to the increase in warehouse staff.

- By moving the focus of the business to increasing sales, these sales may be made at all costs, with large discounts (affecting the gross profit) and/or risking higher bad debt levels. Controls need to be in place to ensure that sales staff are following company policies regarding discounting and offering credit.

- Flexing the budget will give a more useful figure for costs and revenues to compare with the actual costs and revenues generated. These variances will help to identify where sales are being made at the expense of profits caused by heavy discounting by sales staff.

- The company's profit has decreased, yet the corporation tax charge has risen. This may suggest issues regarding the computation of the tax during the year. There may be a lack of knowledge remaining in the financial department to complete the tax return correctly, and taking advantage of any reliefs.

(b)

- The company has increased its revenues by 12% and its gross profit by 16% which in a competitive market is very good. However, increased operating expenses have resulted in a reduction in operating profits of 20%.

- The gross margin is very high; this is not abnormal in this sector, especially for software (although the margin is high for hardware), but it may also be the result of errors, due to the staff turnover.

- Total expenses as a percentage of revenue have increased substantially in 20X3 (47%) compared with expenses in 20X2 (30%). The result of this has seen operating profit as a percentage of revenue reducing significantly year on year from 48% (20X2) to 34% (20X3).

- The increase in the distribution costs as a percentage of revenue (an increase of 5%) may reflect inefficiencies in the method of distribution in an industry that separates these functions.

- The administrative expenses as a percentage of revenue have halved from 13% to 7%, although they do not represent a significant amount in absolute terms. This is possibly due to the reduction in financial and administrative staff during the year.

- The increase in the selling expenses as a percentage of revenue by 18% may be as a result of the need for the company to spend more on advertising and the hiring of new sales staff.

- The reduction in profit before tax and the increased tax charge have resulted in a reduction in profit after tax of 43%.

- Total dividends have increased, despite the lower profits. This may be due to pressure from shareholders or a lack of investment in the business (by reinvesting profits made) as a Board of Directors decision.

Chapter 5 – Ratio analysis: Accounting Systems and Controls/Financial Statements of Limited Companies/Management Accounting: Decision and Control

Task 5.1

	✓
Receivables days + Inventory days – Payables days	✓
Receivables days + Payables days – Inventory days	
Inventory days + Receivables days + Payables days	
Inventory days – Receivables days – Payables days	

Task 5.2

(a)

	✓
Understandability	
Relevance	✓
Comparability	
Faithful representation	✓

(b)

Income is defined as:

'Increases in economic benefits during the accounting period in the form of inflows or enhancements of assets or decreases of liabilities that result in increases in equity, other than those relating to contributions from equity participants'.

Task 5.3

(a)

Return on equity	Profit after tax/Total equity × 100
Acid test ratio	(Current assets − Inventories)/Current liabilities
Inventory holding period	Inventories/Cost of sales × 365
Asset turnover (net assets)	Revenue/(Total assets − Current liabilities)
Gearing	Non-current liabilities/(Total equity + Non-current liabilities) × 100

(b) Ratios:

Ratio	Calculation	Working
Return on equity	**18.1%**	5,136/28,326
Acid test ratio	**0.9:1**	(13,192 − 6,724)/7,258
Inventory holding period	**58.3 days**	6,724/42,126 × 365
Asset turnover (net assets)	**1.2 times**	58,914/(55,984 − 7,258)
Gearing	**41.9%**	20,400/(28,326 + 20,400)

Task 5.4

(a)

> **Current ratio**
>
> - Current ratio is better than the industry average
> - Poole Ltd has more current assets available to meet its current liabilities/is more solvent
> - However, the ratio looks to be too high and indicates less efficient management of working capital
> - It may have higher levels of receivables, inventories or cash and cash equivalents/lower payables

Inventory turnover

- Inventory turnover is better than the industry average

- Poole Ltd is selling its inventories slightly more quickly as compared to the industry average

- Could be due to more effective inventory management systems or the company might have reduced its selling prices or employed better marketing techniques

- Leads to lower storage costs and there is less risk of stock obsolescence

Trade receivables collection period

- Trade receivables collection period is worse than the industry average

- Poole Ltd is taking longer to collect debts

- This is bad for cash flow

- Could be due to poor credit control procedures

- May just be offering longer credit terms to boost sales

- Could indicate the presence of irrecoverable debts

Trade payables payment period

- Trade payables payment period may be considered to be better than the industry average (if linked to supplier goodwill) or worse (if linked to cash flow)

- Poole Ltd is paying its trade suppliers sooner

- This is bad for cash flow

- This is good for supplier goodwill

- It may have negotiated additional settlement discounts with suppliers

- Suppliers may have dictated shorter payment terms

(b)

Collect debts more quickly/reduce trade receivable days, eg improve debt collection procedures, reduce credit periods

Problem: possible loss of customers

Increase the length of time taken to pay suppliers/increase trade payable days, eg negotiate extended credit terms, improve payment procedures

Problem: may lose supplier goodwill/settlement discounts

> Increase the inventory turnover by reducing the inventory holding
>
> Problem: run the risk of a stock-out, which in turn, may reduce customer goodwill

Task 5.5

(a)

	✓
Financial perspectives of the company, such as profit margins	✓
Supplier perspectives, such as the number of supplier complaints	
Customer perspectives of the company, such as number of repeat orders	✓

The four perspectives of the Balanced Scorecard are: customer, financial, innovation and learning, and internal perspectives.

(b)

Abbas Ltd Balanced Scorecard	Year ended 31 Dec 20X4	Year ended 31 Dec 20X5	Working
Profitability and gearing:			
Gross profit %	54.3%	50.5%	8,640/17,120 × 100
Operating profit %	12.5%	12.6%	2,150/17,120 × 100
Return on capital employed	23.9%	26.0%	2,150/(7,190 + 1,070) × 100
Gearing	30.1%	13.0%	1070/(7190 + 1070) × 100
Liquidity ratios:			
Current ratio	2.9:1	2.6:1	(10,310 – 5,060)/(1,670 + 380)
Acid test/quick ratio	1.3:1	1.1:1	(2,010 + 340)/(1,670 + 380)

Abbas Ltd Balanced Scorecard	Year ended 31 Dec 20X4	Year ended 31 Dec 20X5	Working
Working capital days:			
Inventory holding period	119 days	125 days	2,900/8,480 × 365
Trade receivables collection period	41 days	43 days	2,010/17,120 × 365
Trade payables payment period	55 days	72 days	1,670/8,480 × 365
Working capital cycle	105 days	96 days	125 + 43 − 72

(c) (i) Profitability

	✓
This has been a year of steady, if unspectacular, progress. Although profitability has dipped, the return on capital employed has been kept under control.	
The profitability ratios give cause for concern. The small increase in sales revenue has not improved the gross profit percentage. Operating expenses have increased, reducing operating profit and return on capital employed.	
The ratios give mixed messages. Some have improved and some have deteriorated. Further investigation is required.	✓

(ii) Gearing

	✓
The decreased gearing ratio is due to the repayment of non-current liabilities.	✓
It is likely that the interest cover ratio has decreased.	
The increased gearing ratio shows that the company has become more risky.	

(iii) **Liquidity**

	✓
Both ratios have deteriorated which indicates that the company is less solvent than last year, however both ratios still fall within an acceptable level.	✓
Both ratios remain quite high, which may indicate that working capital is not being used effectively.	
Some liquidity ratios have improved and some have deteriorated. Further investigation is required to understand whether liquidity is improving.	

(iv) **Working capital**

	✓
The working capital cycle has worsened. The inventory holding period has improved but the other ratios indicate a lack of financial control.	
There is a welcome improvement in the working capital cycle, mainly due to the change in the payment period for payables.	✓
The working capital cycle is worse than a year ago because of the increased revenue.	

(v) **Overall performance**

	✓
Profitability has declined in 20X5. However, the gearing and liquidity measures show an improving financial position.	
20X5 has been a bad year. Profitability has declined and finances are coming under pressure.	
Steady progress has been made in 20X5. The ratios show that the company is being better managed.	✓

Task 5.6

> ### Increase in the current ratio
>
> This may indicate increased inventory, cash or receivable levels. The implications of this may be that the company is expanding, or alternatively that it is experiencing trading difficulties and is unable to sell its inventory or to collect its receivables. An increase may also be due to a decrease in trade payables or other current liabilities.
>
> ### Decrease in gross profit margin
>
> This may indicate that the cost of raw materials or bought-in goods has increased, or that discounts or selling prices have decreased. This may not be a bad thing if the reason for this is an overall increase in turnover.
>
> ### Increase in inventory holding period
>
> An increase in inventory holding period may indicate that the company is unable to sell its inventory. An increase can also indicate that the company is expecting additional sales, or simply that the business is expanding. Many businesses are cyclical and increases and decreases are to be expected.
>
> ### An increase in gearing
>
> Gearing is the relationship between equity and borrowings. A high level of gearing generally indicates that the company has a high level of borrowings and must pay fixed interest on the borrowings. This means that there is less available for shareholders but it may also mean that the company is expanding, which means greater returns for shareholders in the future. A high gearing ratio may mean that the company is at risk of financial problems.

Task 5.7

(a)

	✓
An architectural practice	
A supermarket	
An estate agent	
A manufacturer	✓

The high inventory turnover rules out the estate agency and architectural practice. Supermarkets can also have a high inventory turnover, but tend to operate on low profit margin.

(b)

	✓
5.1%	✓
4.7%	
6.6%	
6%	

	£000
Profit before interest and tax	230 %
Capital employed (3,500 + 1,000)	4,500
	= 5.1%

(c)

	✓
Reducing the receivables collection period	
Reducing the inventory holding period	
Reducing the payables payment period	✓
Reducing time taken to produce goods	

This will reduce working capital and means that it will take longer to build up working capital needed for production. The other options will all speed up the operating cycle.

(d)

	✓
3.9%	✓
7.6%	
16.1%	
7.1%	

Operating profit margin is a component of ROCE, so 16.3%/4.12 = 3.9%

Task 5.8

(a)

	Peas	Carrots
ROCE	$= \dfrac{(1500 - 240) \times 100}{(5500 + 3000)}$ $= 14.8\%$	$= \dfrac{(2500 - 500) \times 100}{(2800 + 6200)}$ $= 22.2\%$
Gross profit margin	$= 1500/12000 \times 100$ $= 12.5\%$	$= 2500/20500 \times 100$ $= 12.2\%$
Operating profit margin	$= \dfrac{(1500 - 240) \times 100}{12000}$ $= 10.5\%$	$= \dfrac{(2500 - 500) \times 100}{20,500}$ $= 9.8\%$
Current ratio	$= 5000/4100$ $= 1.2{:}1$	$= 7300/5700$ $= 1.3{:}1$
Closing inventory holding period	$= \dfrac{2000}{10500} \times 365$ $= 70$ days	$= \dfrac{3600}{18000} \times 365$ $= 73$ days
Trade receivables collection period	$= \dfrac{2400}{12000} \times 365$ $= 73$ days	$= \dfrac{3700}{20500} \times 365$ $= 66$ days
Trade payables payment period	$= \dfrac{3100}{10500} \times 365$ $= 108$ days	$= \dfrac{3800}{18000} \times 365$ $= 77$ days
Gearing	$= \dfrac{3000 \times 100}{(3000+5500)}$ $= 35.3\%$	$= \dfrac{6200 \times 100}{(6200 + 2800)}$ $= 68.9\%$
Interest cover	$= \dfrac{(1050 + 210)}{210}$ $= 6$ times	$= \dfrac{(1400 + 600)}{600}$ $= 3.3$ times
Dividend cover	$= 900/250$ $= 3.6$ times	$= 1000/700$ $= 1.4$ times

(b) Profitability

Carrots has an ROCE 50% higher than Peas, which is driven by the higher sales and operating profits values. Carrots' operating profit is 60% higher than Peas' operating profit. They both have a similar capital employed. This means that Carrots is more efficient at using its resources to generate income.

The gross profit margins and operating profit margins are very similar, meaning that they are equally good at controlling their costs.

Gearing

Carrots has approximately double the gearing of Peas, due to its higher borrowings. Carrots' interest cover is 3.3 times compared to six times for Peas, making its level of risk higher.

In a bad year Carrots could have trouble servicing its debts and have nothing left to pay to shareholders.

However, the fact that Carrots has chosen to operate with a higher level of gearing rather than raise funds from a share issue also increases the potential return to shareholders.

Liquidity

Peas and Carrots have broadly similar current ratios, but showing a slightly higher level of risk in the case of Carrots. Carrots is also running an overdraft while Peas has a positive cash balance.

Peas is pursuing its receivables slightly less aggressively than Carrots, but taking significantly longer to pay its suppliers.

As this does not appear to be due to shortage of cash, it must be due to Peas being able to negotiate more favourable terms than Carrots.

Summary

Carrots has a higher revenue than Peas and a policy of paying out most of its earnings to shareholders. This makes it an attractive proposition from a shareholder viewpoint.

However, if its revenue were to fall, there would be little left to distribute. This is the risk and return of a highly geared company.

Carrots is already running an overdraft and so has no cash to invest in any more plant and equipment. In the light of this, its dividend policy is not particularly wise. Peas has a lower revenue and a much more conservative dividend policy but may be a better long-term investment.

Forrest's decision will probably depend upon its attitude to risk and the relative purchase prices of Peas and Carrots.

●●

Task 5.9

(a)

	20X1	20X0
Net profit %	= 3000/25500 × 100 = 11.8%	= 2500/17250 × 100 = 14.5%
Operating profit %	= 5900/25500 × 100 = 23.1%	= 3600/17250 × 100 = 20.9%
Gross profit %	= 10700/25500 × 100 = 42%	= 6900/17250 × 100 = 40%
ROCE	= 5900/18500 × 100 = 31.9%	= 3600/9250 × 100 = 38.9%
ROE	= 3000/9500 = 31.6%	= 2500/7250 = 34.5%
Gearing	= 9000/(9000 + 9500) × 100 = 48.7%	= 2000/(2000 + 7250) × 100 = 21.6%
Interest cover	= 5900/650 = 9.1 times	= 3600/100 = 36 times
Current ratio	= 6000/5200 = 1.2:1	= 7200/3350 = 2.2: 1
Quick ratio	= (6000 – 3600)/5200 = 0.5:1	= (7200 – 1800)/3350 = 1.6:1

(b) Profitability

Revenue has increased by 48% while profit for the year has only increased by 20%. However, on closer inspection, we can see that this is to a large degree attributable to the tax charge for the year. The pre-tax profit has increased by 50%, which is in line with the increased revenue.

We do not have a breakdown of the tax charge but it could include underpayments in previous years, which distorts the trading results.

The gross profit margin and operating profit margin are very similar to the prior year, both showing a slight improvement.

There has been a significant increase in capital employed during the year ended 31.12. 20X1. There is an additional £12.3 million in non-current assets, financed from a new issue of 8% loan notes. This has had the effect of reducing the return on capital employed slightly, but not nearly as much as would be expected, indicating that the investment is already producing returns.

The return on equity is skewed by the tax charge, without which, it would be showing a slight increase due to the increased profits.

Gearing

The increase in loan capital does have significance for shareholders. The interest charge has increased from £100,000 to £650,000, which reduces the amount available for dividends.

Gearing has increased significantly. The rate that TTP has to offer to loan note holders has already increased from 5% to 8%. If it required further borrowing, with this high gearing, it would have to pay substantially more.

Shares in TTP have become a riskier investment. One indicator of this is the interest cover, which has fallen from 36 times to 9 times.

Liquidity

The area in which there is most cause for concern is liquidity. Cash has fallen by £4.2 million and the company is now running an overdraft.

It has tax to pay of £2.2 million and this will incur penalties if it is not paid on time. The current ratio has declined from 2.1:1 to 1.2:1 and the quick ratio, which indicates the immediate cash situation, shows a fall from 1.6:1 to 0.5:1, which is a dangerous position to be in.

Summary

Overall, shareholders should be reassured that TTP is profitable and expanding. The company has perhaps overstretched itself and significantly raised its gearing, but it is to be hoped that the investment for which this cash was presumably used will bring in future returns, which should help with the liquidity issues, as long as the company manages to stay solvent until then.

Chapter 6 – Internal controls: Accounting Systems and Controls/Financial Statements of Limited Companies/Management Accounting: Budgeting/Management Accounting: Decision and Control

Task 6.1

Rees Ltd's plan is | an incremental | change.

The fact that the time of Rees Ltd's accounting staff will be freed up by not having to complete cheques by hand is | a tangible benefit of the change | .

Task 6.2

(a) A key strength is that no customer order for even a single high value item is accepted without authorisation by the sales manager, and higher value orders must also be approved by the sales director. This reduces the exposure of the company to incurring the cost of making bespoke furniture to customer order and then finding that it is not actually a valid sale.

(b) There does not appear to be a firm price agreed with the customer for the furniture ordered. It may be that the uncertainty surrounds discounts or the firm price is agreed once production have priced each job. If this is the case then the procedures need to be explicit on this point. If in fact there is no firm price agreed then the business is exposed to the risk that the customer, on receipt of the goods, refuses to pay or only pays a smaller sum than the company is due.

(c) As well as a firm price being agreed with the customer at the time the order is taken, and this being approved by the sales manager and sales director where relevant, the company should get the customer to pay a deposit to the company. This will give it more assurance that the furniture will be accepted and fully paid for once delivered. It will also improve the company's working capital cycle.

Task 6.3

(a) The procedures include a robust process for ensuring that orders are taken only from new customers who represent a good credit risk. It is also a strength that, depending on the outcome of the checks, the sales manager has the discretion to require payment in full upfront or payment on credit terms. The business benefits from these in that there should be no irrecoverable debts, and cash flow should be maintained.

(b) It is possibly a weakness that credit checks etc are only performed on new customers. Existing customers should also be reviewed, depending on their history with the company and the length of time since they last bought. As it is the company may still be exposed to poor payment.

It is a serious weakness that the accounts receivable clerk creates and posts invoices, has sole discretion to issue credit notes, and identifies and posts receipts. This lack of segregation of duties creates a serious risk of fraud by the clerk, alone or in collusion with a customer. The sales manager should authorise invoices and credit notes, and someone else should be responsible for identifying receipts and posting them.

(c) It seems strange that a credit customer is offered 15% discount for early payment, when no such discount is offered to customers who must pay in advance. It is possible that orders are being lost through this policy, or alternatively that revenue for an agreed sale is being lost unnecessarily. The company could consider offering a discount to cash customers, and a reduced discount to early-paying credit customers.

....

Task 6.4

(a) **(i)** The highest value items – for production and for capital expenditure – require senior management authority before being ordered, and all purchases except the most minor require proper purchase orders. Staff understand therefore that proper procedures must be followed before items can be purchased, which reduces the risk of unnecessary items being bought by the company or that staff will purchase items for themselves at the company's expense.

(ii) A coherent approach is taken towards negotiating credit terms with suppliers, which benefits the company's cash flow and planning.

(b) **(i)** It appears items can be purchased from suppliers without a price having been agreed upon. This introduces unnecessary uncertainty into the company's costs and cash flows, and may mean that some items that should be authorised are bought without authority. The remedy is that no purchase orders may be raised without an agreed price being stated on them.

(ii) There is no security over the purchase order forms, so in theory any staff member or other person may obtain a form and purchase items to the account of Sleeptight Ltd. This means the company may be liable to pay for items it has not received or does not want. Purchases should not be allowed to proceed unless a purchase order number, taken from the purchase order book which is kept securely, is notified to the supplier.

(iii) Outside of production materials and capital expenditure there is no need for higher authority and no cash limit on an individual purchase. In theory this could result in an entire budget being spent inappropriately. All purchases above a certain amount should be authorised by the finance director.

(c) Negotiations by the purchasing manager with suppliers seem to focus only on how long the company can take to pay. There is an opportunity to expand the role of the purchasing manager to (1) guide and authorise budget holders in their purchases and (2) negotiate prices, delivery terms and discounts with existing and new suppliers.

Task 6.5

(a) There appears to be good co-ordination between ordering and receiving goods, with Goods Inwards expecting receipts since they have the copy orders. They also check the goods before agreeing they are acceptable by signing the documentation and forwarding to accounts so the subsequent invoice can be recorded. These strengths help to ensure that only goods ordered are received, recorded and paid for, and those goods are of acceptable quality. This will help the company's profits.

(b) There is a serious lack of segregation of duties in the accounting function as the same person (the accounts payable clerk) records invoices, asks for credit notes, decides on payment and makes payment. This increases the risk that through collusion or alone, the clerk could engage in fraud, or could make mistakes that are not corrected (especially overpaying, which is unlikely to be complained about by suppliers). At least one other person should be involved in processing, recording, authorising and paying invoices. A third person should be responsible for reviewing figures and procedures.

Task 6.6

(a) The company maintains a good system of recording and validating production hours spent on individual items of furniture via the job sheets completed by production workers and checked by supervisors. This means the company has a good idea of how much in terms of labour it costs to produce each item, so the company can ensure it covers its costs for each item.

(b) **(i)** There is no check over signing in and out by production workers. As the payroll clerk prepares wages on the basis of the signing-in book, this means that the company may be paying for hours not worked. In addition the signing-in book should be kept in a secure place and should be checked and authorised by managers/supervisors.

(ii) There is no segregation of duties with regard to payroll accounting, so the payroll clerk may be making mistakes/committing fraud without any checks. In particular the accounts manager should be responsible for authorising amendments to standing data, especially for leavers and joiners, for reviewing the reconciliation of the wages control account, and for authorising or processing bank transfers.

(c) The hours recorded in the signing-in book could be reconciled to the hours of productive work recorded on the job sheets. This would help as a sense check on both records and would also help to identify idle time.

Task 6.7

Transaction stream	Risk	Control objective	Control activity
Purchasing	Company pays for goods it does not receive	Ensure all payments are only made for goods actually received, and which are in accordance with the order.	Examine goods in for quality and quantity and reconcile the goods to the original order. Issue a goods received note, which is matched to the invoice prior to payment.
Sales	Sales recorded late so fines incurred from HMRC with respect to VAT	Record invoices in the correct time period	Implement cut-off procedures

Transaction stream	Risk	Control objective	Control activity
Payroll	Company overpays	Pay employees the correct, authorised gross pay	Refer to standing data when calculating wages and salaries. Implement good timekeeping controls, which are used in the wages calculation.

Task 6.8

(a) The original budgeted profit was £73,300 based on budgeted sales of 178,000 units. The actual profit of £80,100 was achieved by selling 192,000 units, some 8% higher sales volume than budgeted.

The original budgeted sales price was £7.20 per unit, while the actual sales price achieved was slightly less at £7.17 per unit.

The main factor leading to the increase in profit was therefore the significant increase in sales volume which more than compensated for the fall in price achieved.

Some categories of costs, eg labour and administration, reported favourable variances in the operating report, which additionally contributed to the increase in profit.

(b) It is possible that there may have been errors in the prices charged to customers. Internal controls over the use of price lists when invoicing, and the completeness of sales recording, should be checked.

Similarly, there may have been errors in processing and recording purchases underlying the costs, or there may have been poor purchasing procedures so that the best deal on prices was not secured.

Task 6.9

Transaction stream	Risk	Control objective	Control activity
Payroll	Company incurs fines from HMRC	Ensure all deductions have been properly calculated and authorised	Reconcile total pay and deductions in wages control account regularly. Ensure up-to-date tax codes are used for each employee.
Sales	Custom lost through chasing payments already made by the customer	Bank and record all money received accurately	Reconcile the bank account regularly and ensure all receipts are allocated to the correct sales ledger account.
Purchasing	Company pays the wrong supplier	Record invoices in the correct purchases ledger account	Reconcile supplier statements with the purchases ledger accounts.

Task 6.10

(a) Tangible costs are easily identified, quantifiable costs of the change for example buying a new software package. These costs can be calculated based on evidence such as invoices or timesheets. Tangible costs associated with training might include:

- Cost of training course

- Cost of lost chargeable hours (as the staff will not be working on clients' accounts)

- Travel expenses to the training provider

Intangible costs are costs of the change that are more difficult to identify and quantify eg the cost of lost custom as customers go elsewhere during the disruption caused by the change. These might include:

- Other staff feeling discontent as new staff are provided with training which they did not have

- Loss of efficiency as new staff's induction is extended and therefore they are not available for client work

- Client dissatisfaction at delays in completion of work due to staff not being available

(b) Costs of the system

- Cost of staff time – preparing the data for migration to the new system and assisting the software contractors.

- The cost of the 'learning curve' whereby staff will be slower initially on the new software whilst they practise using it. There may initially be teething problems eg being able to use the reports and understanding what the system can and cannot do.

- Cost of implementing the new system:

  - Full system initial cost £10,800
  - Annual ongoing cost £3,300

- Having an integrated system would lead to reduced calculation errors, simpler and faster online reporting (to HM Revenue and Customs for PAYE) and closer monitoring of the inventory chain.

- Initial training costs will be dependent on how many staff will be trained. If at least 10 staff members (including both directors) are trained, it would be cost effective to have an in-house training programme. The financial outlay would be the same as sending all 10 to college, but it would reduce the travel expenses.

- The downside would be that 10 people would be unavailable to perform business work on the day of training.

- Crachett & Co may consider to send selected members of staff to college to complete the learning, for example five staff members costing £275 each, total cost of £1,375, and these staff could act as 'champions' and assist those members of staff who will complete the online training (such as more restricted users, maybe more junior members of the team or administration or support staff).

- The training programme selected will need to be considered in terms of the financial costs, plus the opportunity costs of staff being unavailable to undertake client work.

- Timing of the change onto the new software would need to be considered as need to think about any downtime from the system, the training time especially in the busy seasons around Christmas and March year ends.

- Staff discontent amongst those not chosen to receive training on the new system. Additionally some staff may get different levels of training, such as some going to college for the course and others completing the online course. This may lower staff morale and productivity.

- Staff completing the online course, there is a risk that they will not complete the training in line with the launch of the new system. The licence allows six months access, so staff using the online training will need to be reviewed to ensure they have completed it on time.

Workings

Training costs

£2,700 for 15 people is £180 per person

For the same outlay, albeit training people at college, this is £275 per person. Therefore it is cost effective if 10 people at least are trained at the in-house course (£2,700/275 = 9.8).

Benefits of the system

- Staff are better trained in basic knowledge and skills so they are more efficient.

- Staff morale improves as they feel valued due to the investment in training them, increasing their motivation.

- Customers see well-trained and knowledgeable staff so the company's reputation is enhanced, leading to more repeat custom and recommendations from satisfied customers.

- If everyone is trained at the same time (such as using the in-house training), staff can discuss issues with each other rather than struggling on alone. It will act as a team building exercise and improve morale.

- More efficient working practices, as the bookkeeping, financial reporting and tax reporting will be integrated in the new system, leading to fewer errors and missing information. This could improve profit margins as staff will take less time to complete the client work.

Conclusion

The partners of Crachett & Co should consider the long term as well as the short term implications of the new software. The new software will enable the firm to become more efficient and also ensuring all updates to the software are completed in a timely manner. Although the costs are initially high (financially and in terms of staff time and effort), the longer term efficiencies and the ability to grow the business will enable Crachett & Co to benefit in the long term.

AAT AQ2016 PRACTICE ASSESSMENT 1
LEVEL 4 SYNOPTIC ASSESSMENT

Time allowed: 3 hours

The AAT may call the assessments on their website, under study support resources, either a 'practice assessment' or 'sample assessment'.

Level 4 Synoptic Assessment
AAT practice assessment 1

Company background and history

SL Products Ltd (SLP) is a market-leading manufacturing business supplying advanced technological electronics to a number of companies around the world.

The company operates through a manufacturing division and a sales division. The manufacturing division supplies electronics to the sales division, which sells both its own manufactured product and other complementary products that it buys in from third parties.

SLP has its head office on an industrial estate in Manchester, where its management team and accounts department are both based. Its main manufacturing plant is also on this site, as is the sales division's offices and large central warehouse.

SLP was established 10 years ago by three of its four controlling shareholders, Shaun Murphy, Colin Smith and Cynthia Moss. Six years ago they sold most of their shareholding in the business, and now do not have a controlling interest.

Louise Harding was brought into the company and joined the board as Finance Director just over 18 months ago when the other directors and main shareholders realised the company's urgent need to have more high-level professional accounting expertise.

Over the past 10 years, the company has grown rapidly and in the year ended 31 December 20X1 it had a turnover of £20 million. It also now employs around 400 full-time equivalent employees. However, profits from operations have fallen in recent years.

In an attempt to improve profitability, SLP has recently acquired a controlling interest in Merville Ltd, a small manufacturing business that offers unique, patented products that are complementary to those manufactured by SLP. Merville Ltd has prepared initial accounts for its first year of trading under the control of SLP.

A management bonus is linked to these results but it has not yet been authorised for payment by SLP's remuneration committee.

SLP's mission statement

We aim to be a market-focused business that specialises in the research, manufacture and distribution of passive electronic components.

Our priorities are quality, service and providing a product range at the cutting-edge of technology. We offer our customers cost effective products of the highest quality.

We aim to develop long-term relationships with all our stakeholders and deal with suppliers, customers and our staff with the highest levels of integrity.

Developments in the electronics market

During the past few years, the company has been feeling the effects of a recession. Intense competition from overseas manufacturers, made worse by the strength of the pound, has led to a progressive lowering of market prices within the areas in which SLP operates.

It is also becoming increasingly difficult for small companies like SLP to compete with the Research and Development (R&D) budgets available to larger businesses. As the pace of technological change in electronics has accelerated, the company's product range has gradually lost the lead it once had in cutting-edge technology.

The directors have now reluctantly decided that they may be forced to downsize some parts of the business that they spent the past 10 years building up. On the other hand, as they are unable to outspend their bigger competitors on R&D, they are looking to acquire stakes in companies like Merville Ltd to fill the resulting gaps in their product range.

SLP's strategic planning and control

When Louise Harding joined SLP, she suggested that they need to view it from different perspectives rather than just focus on its financial results. The directors and the controlling shareholders agreed to develop measures, collect data and judge the company's performance relative to each of these perspectives. These measures have now been in place for a full year and have just been reviewed.

Perspective 1

The first perspective involves employee training and having corporate cultural attitudes that relate to both individual and corporate self-improvement. In an organisation, such as SLP, that relies on problem solving and creative thinking, its people are an important resource. In a market characterised by rapid technological change, it is necessary for staff to be in a continuous learning mode.

Measures were put into place to focus training and development funds where they could help the most.

This perspective, which recognises that 'learning' is more than 'training', also considers aspects such as the effectiveness of mentoring within the organisation, as well as the ease of communication among workers that allows them to get help with a problem easily, when needed.

In general, the first year's results show that the company has performed well in relation to this perspective.

Perspective 2

The second perspective refers to internal business processes. Measures based on this perspective allow the directors to see how well their business is running, and

whether its products and services conform to customer requirements (as per its mission statement).

Those who know these processes most intimately, namely the various line managers within SLP, carefully designed these measures.

In general, the first year's results show that the company has performed poorly in relation to this perspective. This is because the business is gradually losing its technological lead in several of its products.

Perspective 3

The third perspective relates to how SLP's customers view the business. Cynthia Moss has stressed the importance of customer focus and customer satisfaction. She has emphasised that these are leading indicators; if customers are not satisfied, they will eventually find other suppliers that will meet their needs better. Poor performance on this perspective is therefore a key indicator of future decline, even though the current financial results may still look reasonable.

To develop measures for customer satisfaction, SLP examined its customers both in terms of the kinds of customers they are, and the kinds of products that they are buying from SLP.

The first year's results indicate that customers were generally satisfied with the customer care and service, but were less satisfied with some of the older products in the product range that were overdue for replacement.

Interestingly, customers were generally more satisfied with the bought-in products being sold by the sales division than those manufactured in-house by SLP itself. There was considerable interest in the new products manufactured by Merville Ltd.

Perspective 4

The fourth and final perspective is the traditional outlook using financial data. Louise Harding instigated the use of more accurate and timely monthly management accounts immediately after she was appointed. She argued that the previous focus on only financial data had led to an "unbalanced" situation with no attention having been paid to the real drivers of business performance.

The financial results continue to show falling profits which the other three perspectives help to explain.

Strategy-mapping

SLP has used the first year's results to carry out a strategy-mapping exercise (strategy maps are communication tools used to tell a story of how value is created for the organisation. They show a logical, step by step connection between strategic objectives in the form of causes and effects).

Generally speaking, improving performance in the objectives from the first of SLP's perspectives will enable it to improve its internal processes. This will enable it to

improve its results for customer satisfaction and eventually its financial performance.

This implies that SLP needs to reallocate resources towards increasing its R&D spend which will, in turn, redirect its internal processes towards new product development. This should result in improved customer satisfaction and retention, with the final outcome being increased profitability.

Some of the directors, however, believe that the root cause of SLP's problems lies in exactly the matters that are under the Finance Director's direct control, ie the problems are due to poor internal controls and systemic weaknesses. The directors also point out that they will struggle to finance any increase in R&D.

At this point in time, the board is divided and uncertain how best to proceed.

Staff

SLP's key personnel are as follows:

Managing director	Shaun Murphy
Finance director	Louise Harding
Production director	Colin Smith
Sales director	Cynthia Moss
Chief accountant	Sue Hughes
Purchasing manager	Tony Clark
Warehouse manager	Robert Utley
Credit controller	Ray Massey
Accounts payable clerk	Liz Hall
Accounts receivable clerk	Matthew Tunnock
General accounts clerk and cashier	Hina Khan
Payroll clerk	Jane Patel

SLP's financial statements

The financial statements for SLP for the year ended 31 December 20X1 show that the company had a turnover of £20 million, and made a profit after tax of £960,000.

These accounts do not include the results of Merville Ltd, which was acquired on 1 January 20X2.

SL Products Ltd – Statement of profit or loss for the year ended 31 December 20X1

Continuing operations	£000
Revenue	20,000
Cost of sales	(14,322)
Gross profit	5,678
Operating expenses	(4,413)
Profit from operations	1,265
Finance costs	(47)
Profit before tax	1,218
Tax	(258)
Profit for the period from continuing operations	960

SL Products Ltd – Statement of financial position as at 31 December 20X1

	£000
ASSETS	
Non-current assets	
Property, plant and equipment	4,330
	4,330
Current assets	
Inventories	3,614
Trade receivables	2,976
Cash and cash equivalents	8
	6,598
Total assets	10,928

	£000
EQUITY AND LIABILITIES	
Equity	
Ordinary share capital (£1 shares)	800
Share premium	1,160
Retained earnings	4,065
Total equity	6,025
Non-current liabilities	
Bank loans	1,200
	1,200
Current liabilities	
Trade payables	3,360
Bank overdraft	124
Tax liabilities	219
	3,703
Total liabilities	4,903
Total equity and liabilities	10,928

Task 1 (20 marks)

Louise Harding, the Finance Director of SL Products Ltd has asked you to analyse the published results of a competitor business. Until recently, you were employed by that business. Therefore, you have a detailed understanding of its financial position.

(a) Answer the following questions.

Which of your principles is threatened by this request?

Picklist:

Confidentiality
Objectivity
Professional competence and due care

How should you respond?

[▼]

Picklist:

Base your analysis entirely on the published results
Obtain the competitor's agreement
Refuse to do the analysis

(4 marks)

Hina Khan, the Cashier of SL Products Ltd, is preparing a cash flow forecast. She asks which of the following are cash flow items.

(b) **Show whether each of the following should be included in a cash flow forecast by selecting your answers from the picklist.**

Revaluation of premises

[▼]

Bonus issue of shares in SL Products Ltd

[▼]

Payment of dividend on ordinary shares

[▼]

Write off obsolete inventory

[▼]

Picklist:

Do not include
Include in cash flow

(8 marks)

Liz Hall, the Accounts Payable Clerk, asks for you for advice. She wants to know whether the following errors and discrepancies would be detected by reconciling the accounts payable ledger to its control account.

(c) **Show whether each of the following errors and discrepancies would be detected by reconciling the accounts payable ledger to its control account by selecting your answers from the picklist.**

Errors and discrepancies	Answer
A supplier has been paid for an invoice twice	▾
A supplier invoice has been posted to the wrong supplier account	▾
A cheque payment has been debited to the accounts receivable control account	▾
VAT on some purchases has been omitted from the VAT return	▾
A purchase invoice has been debited to the account of a supplier	▾

Picklist:

Would be detected
Would not be detected

(5 marks)

Liz Hall maintains the accounts payable ledger. Her duties include ensuring the accounts payable ledger agrees to its control account.

(d) **What sort of access should Liz have to the accounts payable control account?**

Picklist:

Full access, including data entry
No access
Read only access

(1 mark)

An inventory count is to take place at SL Products Ltd's financial year end. Sue Hughes, Chief Accountant, is concerned that the inventory value will appear to be too high. She suggests that all inventory receipts in the final week of December should be dated 1 January and that those items should be excluded from the count. The relevant purchase invoices would be posted in the new accounting period.

(e)   Which of the following statements describes this suggestion?

	✓
Acceptable commercial practice	
Unethical 'window dressing'	
Fraud	
Breach of the control environment	

(2 marks)

Task 2 (15 marks)

SL Products Ltd acquired a controlling interest in a small manufacturing business called Merville Ltd on 1 January 20X2.

Unaudited accounts for Merville Ltd's financial year ended 31 December 20X2 have been prepared and an operating budget has been drafted for approval by the directors of SL Products Ltd.

The administration costs for 20X2 include a provision of £21,000 for a profit related management bonus, payable to the directors of Merville Ltd.

You have been asked to review the budget proposal and supporting submission.

Budget submission

The directors of Merville Ltd are pleased to present a budget proposal for 20X3. Actual (unaudited) results for 20X2 are provided for comparison. Your approval of the budget is requested.

Substantial sales growth was achieved in 20X2. We introduced more than a dozen innovative new products. The key features of these products are patented and therefore protected for direct competition. Merville Ltd has a solid customer base.

In 20X3, Merville Ltd will retain its own identity in the market place. In addition, we plan to develop a sales channel through SL Products Ltd and to be promoted in that company's catalogue.

We have 50 products in our catalogue at all stages of the product life cycle. More exciting new products are being planned. We do not feel that it is realistic to try to calculate sales revenue and costs at product level. However, we are confident that we will achieve the budgeted 10% volume growth.

We have not assumed any increase in selling prices because this is difficult to achieve with high-tech products.

In addition to the 10% volume growth, we have allowed 2.5% for cost increases in line with expected inflation.

Operating budget for year ended 31 December 20X3	Unaudited results 20X2	Draft budget 20X3
Sales volume (units)	7,950	8,745
	£	£
Sales revenue	1,128,900	1,241,790
Costs:		
Materials	246,450	277,256
Labour	409,425	460,603
Production overheads	144,690	162,776
Depreciation	46,800	52,650
Marketing	18,640	20,970
Administration	92,600	104,175
Total	958,605	1,078,430
Operating profit	170,295	163,360
Operating profit % to sales	15.1%	13.2%

Prepare a report for the chief accountant of SL Products Ltd in three sections as follows:

(a) Examine the planning assumptions and calculations in the proposed budget and identify any weaknesses.

(5 marks)

(b) **Explain how costs and profitability should be managed in an organisation that manufactures multiple products.**

(5 marks)

(c) **Give your opinion, with reasons, on how well the budget would motivate managers to create sustainable, profitable growth.**

(5 marks)

Task 3 (15 marks)

You have been asked to review the adequacy of the control in SL Products Ltd's purchasing procedures. Your review has established the following information.

The company operates an integrated accounting system which includes a purchase accounting module. Tony Clark, the Purchasing Manager, is responsible for managing purchasing activities.

Ordering and receipt:

- All purchases, except petty cash items, must be documented on an official purchase order. The order should state the agreed price, if known.

- All departments are provided with books of pre-numbered order forms. These books can be obtained from the stationery store.

- Orders for production materials and items for resale must be signed by Robert Utley, the warehouse manager.

- Capital expenditure orders must be signed by Louise Harding, the finance director.

- There is no cash limit for purchase orders provided that they are within the approved budget.

- Other orders must be signed by the relevant budget holders.

- Four copies of the order form are printed. Once signed, the original is sent to the supplier. A copy printed on yellow paper is sent to Liz Hall, the accounts payable clerk. Two further copies, printed on pink and green paper, are retained by the individual who raised the order.

- When the goods or service(s) are received, the individual who raised the order signs the green copy and sends it to Liz Hall. This individual retains the pink copy for their files.

New suppliers:

- New suppliers are contacted by Tony Clark. He provides a trade reference and banking details and requests credit terms.

- He usually requests payment terms as either of the following:

    – Two months from the end of the month in which delivery takes place
    – A 5% discount for payment within 21 days of delivery

    However, terms are subject to negotiation.

- Tony enters the agreed supplier details and payment terms into the supplier master file.

Accounting:

- All purchase invoices are checked by Liz Hall. She checks the calculations, matches the invoices to appropriate yellow and green copy orders and clears the invoices for payment.

- Liz posts the cleared invoices to the computerised accounting system.

- Liz takes up queries with suppliers, requesting credit notes when appropriate.

- Invoices are automatically paid as they fall due through the bankers automated clearing system (BACS). Liz authorises one payment run every week.

Complete your review as follows, using the provided answer spaces below:

- **Identify FIVE systemic weaknesses in the company's internal controls for handling purchases on credit.**

- **Explain how each weakness that you have identified could create a problem for the company.**

Note. You are **not** required to make recommendations to change procedures.

No.	Weakness	Potential problem

(15 marks)

Task 4 (15 marks)

Review of product pricing

The latest annual results of SL Products Ltd have confirmed the trend of decline in the gross profit margin. The Board of Directors has asked Cynthia Moss (Sales Director) and Louise Harding (Finance Director) to review the situation and report back with an agreed proposal.

The company operates in a very competitive, high-tech market. It is necessary to create a stream of innovative new products that are as good as, or better than, those marketed by competitors. Meanwhile, older products rapidly go into decline. It is almost impossible to increase the price of a product after it is launched.

Louise proposes that all new products should be priced to give a 30% mark-up over cost. She says, 'we only get one chance to get the price right. Production costs are always rising but we cannot increase our prices. If we launch the products with a 30% mark-up, they will be profitable for a few years.'

Sue Hughes, the chief accountant, has created a simple spreadsheet model to determine the selling prices for new products. She has used this model to calculate the selling price of two new products that are ready for launch.

Pricing spreadsheet

Sue explains that this is a full overhead recovery pricing model.

The variable element of production overheads is equal to 15% of the direct costs. (The direct costs are all variable.) Marketing and administration costs are fixed.

Prices for new products	£ per unit	
	NP1	NP2
Direct cost	18.00	42.00
Production overhead	3.60	8.40
Marketing and administration	5.40	12.60
30% mark-up	8.10	18.90
Selling price	35.10	81.90

Sales Director's response:

Cynthia says that the spreadsheet prices are not competitive.

She knows that the business will suffer if she cannot refresh the product range with new products at attractive prices.

She has compared each of the two products (NP1 and NP2) with competitors' products and has estimated the sales potential at three price levels.

Price levels and estimated annual volumes	NP1		NP2	
	£ each	Volume	£ each	Volume
To undercut competition	21.00	250	52.00	600
Market price	28.00	150	60.00	400
Spreadsheet price	35.10	50	81.90	150

Cynthia asks you to calculate which prices would be most profitable.

(a) For each product calculate the marginal cost per unit and the annual contribution that would be earned at each of the two prices that Cynthia has considered.

Calculation of contribution	NP1 £	NP2 £
Marginal cost per unit (to the nearest penny)		

Annual contribution	£	£
To undercut the competition		
Market price		
Spreadsheet price		

(8 marks)

(b) Select the price that would give the highest contribution to profit for each of the two products.

Product	Best price
NP1	▼
NP2	▼

Picklist:

Market price
Spreadsheet price
To undercut the competition

(2 marks)

(c) **Discuss the possible impact of Louise Harding's proposed policy on the business.**

(5 marks)

Task 5 (20 marks)

Louise Harding, the Finance Director, is preparing a presentation for the Board of Directors. She has asked you to complete a comparative 'score card' of key financial ratios which she will use as part of her presentation.

Relevant data has been extracted from the last two years' accounts. These extracts do not include the results of Merville Ltd.

Extracts from accounts of SL Products Ltd	Year ended 31 December 20X1 £000	Year ended 31 December 20X2 £000
Sales revenue	20,000	20,900
Cost of sales	14,322	15,144
Profit from operations	1,265	470
Assets		
Non-current assets	4,330	4,234
Inventories	3,614	3,908
Trade receivables	2,976	3,032
Cash and equivalents	8	6
Total	**10,928**	**11,180**

Extracts from accounts of SL Products Ltd	Year ended 31 December 20X1 £000	Year ended 31 December 20X2 £000
Equity and Liabilities		
Equity	6,025	5,550
Non-current liabilities	1,200	1,400
Trade payables	3,360	3,730
Bank overdraft	124	260
Tax liabilities	219	240
Total	**10,928**	**11,180**

(a) **Complete the scorecard by calculating the missing ratios.**

SL Products Ltd Scorecard	Year ended 31 Dec 20X1	Year ended 31 Dec 20X2
Profitability and gearing (correct to 1 dp):		
Gross profit %	28.4%	[ ]%
Operating profit %	6.3%	2.2%
Return on capital employed	17.5%	[ ]%
Gearing	16.6%	20.1%
Liquidity ratios (correct to 1 dp):		
Current ratio	1.8:1	[ ]:1
Acid test/quick ratio	0.8:1	[ ]:1
Working capital days (correct to nearest day):		
Inventory holding period	92 days	94 days
Trade receivables collection period	54 days	59 days
Trade payables payment period	86 days	90 days
Working capital cycle	60 days	[ ] days

(10 marks)

(b) **Select the ONE correct observation about each aspect of business performance below.**

Profitability

	✓
This has been a year of steady, if unspectacular, progress. Although profitability has dipped, the return on capital employed has been kept under control.	
The profitability ratios give cause for concern. The small increase in sales revenue has not improved the gross profit percentage. Operating expenses have increased, reducing operating profit and return on capital employed.	
The ratios give mixed messages. Some have improved and some have deteriorated. Further investigation is required.	

(2 marks)

Gearing

	✓
The increased gearing ratio is entirely due to the increase in non-current liabilities.	
It is likely that the interest cover ratio has increased.	
The increased gearing ratio shows that the company has become more risky.	

(2 marks)

Liquidity

	✓
Both ratios have deteriorated which indicates that the company is less solvent.	
Both ratios remain too high, indicating that working capital is not being used effectively.	
Some liquidity ratios have improved and some have deteriorated. Further investigation is required to understand whether liquidity is improving.	

(2 marks)

Working capital

	✓
The working capital cycle has worsened. The inventory holding period has improved but the other ratios indicate a lack of financial control.	
There is a welcome improvement in the working capital cycle, mainly due to the change in the payment period for payables.	
The working capital cycle is worse than a year ago because of the increased cost of sales.	

(2 marks)

Overall performance

	✓
Profitability has declined in 20X2, mainly due to competitive pressures. However, the gearing and liquidity measures show an improving financial position.	
20X2 has been a bad year. Profitability has declined and finances are coming under pressure.	
Steady progress has been made in 20X2. The ratios show that the company is being better managed.	

(2 marks)

....

Task 6 (15 marks)

You have been asked to carry out a review of SL Products Ltd's sales order processing procedure and make recommendations for improvement.

You have interviewed the Sales Director (Cynthia Moss), Credit controller (Ray Massey) and Accounts Receivable Clerk (Matthew Tunnock). Your findings are below.

Catalogue

The 85-page illustrated catalogue is updated and posted to customers in the spring and autumn of each year. The print run is 5,000 copies. An online version is put on the company's website.

Orders can be placed by post, telephone or online if the customer has been granted credit terms. Otherwise, orders will only be accepted by post and must be paid for in advance by cheque (in British pounds). These cheques are cleared before despatch is allowed.

Accounts that are dormant for 18 months are closed. These customers are removed from the catalogue distribution list.

Customer base

80% of sales are made to just 20% of the credit customers.

Most of these sales are repeat orders for some long-established items in the catalogue. 95% of sales, by value, are to credit account customers.

There are 4,210 customers with credit accounts: 4,000 in the UK; 150 in European Union countries and 60 elsewhere around the world. Over the last year, 129 new customers have been granted credit accounts. 608 inactive accounts have been closed.

Sales to customers outside the UK have declined over the last five years and now make up only 7% of total sales.

Credit accounts

Account application forms are sent to new customers by Matthew Tunnock. Trade and bank references are required. When the forms and references are returned, Matthew checks them and drafts a confirmation letter which Ray Massey authorises.

Matthew sends the confirmation letter, a copy of the company's terms of trade and a catalogue to the new credit customer. There is no formal credit limit at this stage. Credit limits are placed on regular late payers.

Most customers settle their accounts within the agreed periods or very soon after. There are very few bad debts.

You are required to identify four features of these procedures: one strength; one weakness; one threat and one opportunity. Do not use the same feature more than once.

(a) Identify ONE strength in these procedures. Explain how the business benefits from this.

(3 marks)

(b) Identify ONE weakness in these procedures. Explain how this damages the business and suggest a remedy.

(4 marks)

(c) Identify an opportunity to improve the procedures. Explain how the procedure should be changed and how the business could benefit.

(4 marks)

(d) Identify ONE threat to the effectiveness of these procedures. Explain how this could damage the business and suggest an action that would reduce the risk.

(4 marks)

AAT AQ2016 PRACTICE ASSESSMENT 1
LEVEL 4 SYNOPTIC ASSESSMENT

ANSWERS

Level 4 Synoptic Assessment
AAT practice assessment 1

Task 1 (20 marks)

(a) **Which of your principles is threatened by this request?**

Confidentiality

How should you respond?

Base your analysis entirely on the published results

(4 marks)

(b) Revaluation of premises

Do not include

Bonus issue of shares in SL Products Ltd

Do not include

Payment of dividend on ordinary shares

Include in cash flow

Write off obsolete inventory

Do not include

(8 marks)

(c) **Show whether each of the following errors and discrepancies would be detected by reconciling the accounts payable ledger to its control account by selecting your answers from the picklist.**

Errors and discrepancies	Answer
A supplier has been paid for an invoice twice	Would not be detected
A supplier invoice has been posted to the wrong supplier account	Would not be detected
A cheque payment has been debited to the accounts receivable control account	Would be detected
VAT on some purchases has been omitted from the VAT return	Would not be detected
A purchase invoice has been debited to the account of a supplier	Would be detected

(d) What sort of access should Liz have to the accounts payable control account?

Read only access

Liz only needs to view the data, so she does not need to change any data and therefore does not need 'full access, including data entry'. However, she needs read access so that she can ensure the accounts payable ledger agrees to its control account. Therefore, 'read only access' is appropriate for her role.

(1 mark)

(e) Which of the following describes this suggestion?

	✓
Acceptable commercial practice	
Unethical 'window dressing'	✓
Fraud	
Breach of the control environment	

(2 marks)

Task 2 (15 marks)

(a) Examine the planning assumptions and calculations in the proposed budget and identify any weaknesses.

The draft budget is based on the assumption of 10% growth in sales volume. No justification is offered for this round figure assumption. I suggest that we need to review recent trends in Merville Ltd's products, look at the potential for the anticipated new products and estimate the likely additional business generated from our own customers. With only 50 current products, this should not be difficult.

The assumption that sales revenue will only grow relative to sales volume is probably pessimistic. Although we are told prices can never be raised, new products should command a healthy margin when launched, particularly as they are patent protected.

All costs have been increased by 12.5% in the draft budget (2.5% for inflation and 10% for growth). There is no reason why fixed costs should increase by more than an appropriate rate for inflation. Each line of costs needs to be considered carefully according to its cost type (variable, fixed, etc) and its own cost pressures.

> In particular, agreement is required about the management bonus. This has been accrued at £21,000 for 20X2 and, in effect, budgeted at £23,625 for 20X3. This has not yet been approved.

(5 marks)

(b) **Explain how costs and profitability should be managed in an organisation that manufactures multiple products.**

> In a multi-product manufacturing organisation it is essential that costs and profitability are reviewed by product. Therefore, a costing system needs to be in place.
>
> A standard costing system has particular advantages in that it is based on calculations of what the costs should be, called standard costs. This is useful for control as variances from these standards can be reported and investigated.
>
> The standard cost of each product can be compared with its selling price to identify profitability.
>
> Standard costs can be calculated for planned new products to inform price setting.

(5 marks)

(c) **Give your opinion, with reasons, on how well the budget would motivate managers to create sustainable, profitable growth.**

> Budgetary control can be a powerful tool to encourage managers and staff to create sustainable, profitable growth. To do this, budgets need to be stretching but achievable.
>
> The proposed Merville Ltd budget has been prepared by its own directors who have a vested interest, in the form of the management bonus, in ensuring that it is easy to achieve. They have not provided sufficient supporting data to enable us to verify that the sales volume and pricing assumptions are stretching.
>
> Increasing all costs, fixed and variable, by 12.5% cannot be justified and creates significant budgetary slack.
>
> I do not believe that this draft budget would motivate Merville Ltd to create sustainable, profitable growth.

(5 marks)

Task 3 (15 marks)

Complete your review as follows, using the provided answer spaces below:

- **Identify five systemic weaknesses in the company's internal controls for handling purchases on credit.**

- **Explain how each weakness that you have identified could create a problem for the company.**

Note to the answer. There are more suggested answers shown below than are required to be given in the task. Awarded 1 mark for identification of the weakness and 2 (with a maximum of 3) for the explanation.

No.	Weakness	Potential problem
1	The purchasing manager appears to have very little involvement in day to day purchasing, apart from negotiating terms with new suppliers.	Failures in the system and system abuses could go unnoticed.
2	No apparent security for order stationery.	Potential for anyone to commit fraud by making purchases for their own use in the company's name.
3	Budget holders and the warehouse manager can raise orders and sign that the goods or services have been received.	There is a potential for fraud as there does not appear to be any check that these purchases are necessary, or even for business use.
4	The procedures do not include any mention of checking that goods and services of the correct standard have been received.	If this is not happening the company could be paying for unsatisfactory supplies.
5	There is no cash limit to purchase orders provided that they are within the approved budget.	Without a second signature on large purchases, there is scope for errors, poor judgement or fraud to be very costly.
6	Orders can be placed without agreeing a price.	The company is in a weak position to negotiate price after the goods or service have been received.

No.	Weakness	Potential problem
7	Lack of authorisation of new accounts.	There should be a policy for choosing new suppliers. Potential for fraud through collusion with suppliers.
8	The terms agreed by Tony Clark are not countersigned.	Potential for fraud through collusion with suppliers.
9	Only one signature is required on purchase orders.	Potential for fraud through collusion with suppliers.
10	Liz Hall checks, clears and arranges payment of invoices.	Potential for fraud through collusion with suppliers.
11	Tony Clark and Liz Hall control all aspects of purchase accounting.	Potential for fraud through collusion.

(15 marks)

Task 4 (15 marks)

(a) **For each product calculate the marginal cost per unit and the annual contribution that would be earned at each of the two prices that Cynthia has considered.**

Calculation of contribution	NP1 £	NP2 £
Marginal cost per unit (to the nearest penny)	20.70	48.30

Working: direct cost + (15% × direct cost)

Annual contribution	£	£
To undercut the competition	75	2,220
Market price	1,095	4,680
Spreadsheet price	720	5,040

(8 marks)

165

(b) **Select the price that would give the highest contribution to profit for each of the two products**

Product	Best price
NP1	Market price
NP2	Spreadsheet price

(2 marks)

(c) **Discuss the possible impact of Louise Harding's proposed policy on the business.**

In theory, any price that is higher than marginal cost will make a contribution and therefore increase profits. The policy generates prices which are greater than total unit cost, including an apportionment of fixed costs. Therefore they should be profitable at any volume of sale.

Despite being profitable, the new policy could be damaging to the business

The pricing policy does not allow the Sales Director to respond to market conditions and find the combination of profit and volume that will optimise contribution.

SLP is in a price competitive business. If new products are not priced competitively they will only sell in small volumes. As ageing products decline they must be replaced by innovative new ones.

The business will go into decline if the product range is not refreshed.

(5 marks)

Task 5 (20 marks)

(a) **Complete the scorecard by calculating the missing ratios.**

SL Products Ltd Scorecard	Year ended 31 Dec 20X1	Year ended 31 Dec 20X2
Profitability and gearing (correct to 1 dp):		
Gross profit %	28.4%	27.5 %
Operating profit %	6.3%	2.2%
Return on capital employed	17.5%	6.8 %

SL Products Ltd Scorecard	Year ended 31 Dec 20X1	Year ended 31 Dec 20X2
Gearing	16.6%	20.1%
Liquidity ratios (correct to 1 dp):		
Current ratio	1.8:1	1.6 :1
Acid test/quick ratio	0.8:1	0.7 :1
Working capital days (correct to nearest day):		
Inventory holding period	92 days	94 days
Trade receivables collection period	54 days	53 days
Trade payables payment period	86 days	90 days
Working capital cycle	60 days	57 days

(10 marks)

(b) **Select the ONE correct observation about each aspect of business performance below.**

Profitability

	✓
This has been a year of steady, if unspectacular, progress. Although profitability has dipped, the return on capital employed has been kept under control.	
The profitability ratios give cause for concern. The small increase in sales revenue has not improved the gross profit percentage. Operating expenses have increased, reducing operating profit and return on capital employed.	✓
The ratios give mixed messages. Some have improved and some have deteriorated. Further investigation is required.	

(2 marks)

Gearing

	✓
The increased gearing ratio is entirely due to the increase in non-current liabilities.	
It is likely that the interest cover ratio has increased.	
The increased gearing ratio shows that the company has become more risky.	✓

(2 marks)

Liquidity

	✓
Both ratios have deteriorated which indicates that the company is less solvent.	✓
Both ratios remain too high, indicating that working capital is not being used effectively.	
Some liquidity ratios have improved and some have deteriorated. Further investigation is required to understand whether liquidity is improving.	

(2 marks)

Working capital

	✓
The working capital cycle has worsened. The inventory holding period has improved but the other ratios indicate a lack of financial control.	
There is a welcome improvement in the working capital cycle, mainly due to the change in the payment period for payables.	✓
The working capital cycle is worse than a year ago because of the increased cost of sales.	

(2 marks)

Overall performance

	✓
Profitability has declined in 20X2, mainly due to competitive pressures. However, the gearing and liquidity measures show an improving financial position.	
20X2 has been a bad year. Profitability has declined and finances are coming under pressure.	✓
Steady progress has been made in 20X2. The ratios show that the company is being better managed.	

(2 marks)

Task 6 (15 marks)

(a) **Identify ONE strength in these procedures. Explain how the business benefits from this.**

> Effective credit control is in place. New applicants for accounts are credit checked and there is routine credit control. This minimises bad debts and assists cash flow.

(3 marks)

(b) **Identify ONE weakness in these procedures. Explain how this damages the business and suggest a remedy.**

> It is not easy for new customers to place orders, particularly from overseas. The requirement to apply for credit terms or to send a cheque through the post is an obstacle to trade and is probably sending potential customers elsewhere. Only 5% of sales are made against cleared cheques.
>
> The account opening procedure needs to be performed electronically. Customers should be able to apply online for a small initial credit limit which can be immediately checked with a credit reference agency. Alternatively, a facility to pay online by credit or debit card when placing an order would be attractive to small businesses and those with a poor credit record.

(4 marks)

(c) **Identify an opportunity to improve the procedures. Explain how the procedure should be changed and how the business could benefit.**

> There appears to be an opportunity to improve relations with customers. Printed catalogues are expensive to produce and distribute and not as effective as targeted electronic communications. Customers could be sent daily electronic mail shots tailored to their own buying records and browsing history. The catalogue could be updated daily.
>
> This could save money and should boost sales.

(4 marks)

(d) **Identify ONE threat to the effectiveness of these procedures. Explain how this could damage the business and suggest an action that would reduce the risk.**

> We operate in a competitive environment. 80% of our sales are made to just 840, or so, customers and consist mainly of repeat orders for established products. We are vulnerable if our competitors offer new or cheaper products to these customers.
>
> We must protect this business by ensuring that we develop or buy the best available products at competitive prices.

(4 marks)

AAT AQ2016 PRACTICE ASSESSMENT 2 LEVEL 4 SYNOPTIC ASSESSMENT

You are advised to attempt the sample assessment online from the AAT website. This will ensure you are prepared for how the assessment will be presented on the AAT's system when you attempt the real assessment. Please access the assessment using the address below:

https://www.aat.org.uk/training/study-support/search

The AAT may call the assessments on their website, under study support resources, either a 'practice assessment' or 'sample assessment'.

Scenario Overview
LEVEL 4 SYNOPTIC ASSESSMENT

Ruby Dale Ltd

For assessments 1 September 2019-31 August 2020

Scenario

Version correct as at 15 May 2019, please check online at www.aat.org.uk to ensure you have the latest version

RUBY DALE LTD

Company background

History

Ruby Dale Ltd is a private limited company based in Manchester, which designs, manufactures, distributes and retails luxury shoes and handbags.

The business began 10 years ago when Ruby Dale, an award winning fashion school graduate, started to sell her bespoke hand-made shoes on the internet on a made to order basis.

Ruby was joined two years later by Jack Carey, an entrepreneur, and together they formed Ruby Dale Ltd. Jack had seen Ruby's shoes featured in a leading fashion magazine and, sensing their wider market appeal, wished to manufacture a ready-to-wear version of the shoes on a much greater scale. They built a factory on an industrial estate in Manchester to make the shoes, and opened their first shop in Manchester in 20X0.

Recent developments

Ruby Dale Ltd has expanded rapidly over the last few years – facilitated by numerous celebrity endorsements – more than doubling the workforce and opening three new shops in London, Paris and New York, one in each location. The company also supplies its products to major high street retailers and independent stores, as well as enabling customers to purchase directly through the company's website. As Ruby Dale Ltd has grown it has diversified its portfolio of products, and now complements its core offering of luxury women's shoes with handbags, men's evening shoes and luxury trainers. The handbag collection in particular now forms an integral part of the business in terms of helping to promote the Ruby Dale lifestyle brand. In the last year, the company has also re-launched the made-to-order service – having originally stopped this when the shoes first started to be mass produced – to allow customers the option of purchasing a product that will be bespoke to them.

Financial performance

Revenue increased by 20% in the year ending 30 September 20X5, with women's shoes – comprising 80% of turnover – being the main driver as the company launched a number of new styles across its product range. Sales to customers in the United Kingdom and Europe largely remained unchanged, due to economic uncertainty caused by political events. Sales to customers in Asia, the USA and the emerging economies, such as Brazil and Russia, experienced strong growth,

assisted by a weaker pound sterling, rising levels of disposable income and a greater brand awareness. Sales to UK customers still remain the company's main market, representing 42% of turnover. The e-commerce part of the business performed particularly well, delivering exceptional sales growth of 34%, as Ruby Dale Ltd introduced new features and technology on the online platform to improve the shopping experience of customers.

Resources

On 30 September 20X5 Ruby Dale Ltd had 160 employees.

Department	Number of staff
Production, storage and distribution	73
Retail	41
Administration	26
Marketing	12
Design and development	8

Apart from 29 employees who work in the company's four shops, the rest are located at Ruby Dale Ltd's headquarters in Manchester, where production is based. Although the site has expanded in order to meet the growing demand for the company's products, it is now starting to reach the limit of its manufacturing capacity with a couple of product lines experiencing temporary stockout shortages in the early part of 20X5. After a comprehensive tendering process, Ruby Dale Ltd made the decision in the latter part of the year to outsource production of its handbags to a manufacturing company located in Asia, its principal area of market growth. Further outsourcing opportunities are also to be considered as the company looks to reduce its cost base and further expand its product range.

Sustainability

Ruby Dale Ltd is committed to sustainable development with regard to the economic, social and environmental aspects of its business.

The company operates a comprehensive training programme for all employees, which allows it to advance workplace safety, productivity and satisfaction. This is especially important given the large influx of new members of staff. It has recently embarked on an apprenticeship scheme to develop the company's designers and managers of the future, and works closely with local schools and colleges to promote interest in the fashion industry and to identify high potential talent. In 20X3, Ruby Dale Ltd set up the Ruby Dale Foundation which sponsors under-privileged children to study fashion at university, as well as raising funds for local community projects.

In relation to the environment, Ruby Dale Ltd is striving to achieve ambitious savings in water, waste and energy. Recent initiatives include the installation of a water recycling system in the factory; removing single-use plastic items such as plastic bags, water bottles and cutlery from all company sites; replacing traditional lighting with LED lights; upgrading the fabric of buildings to improve insulation and boost energy efficiency. In addition, Ruby Dale Ltd has now implemented a scheme whereby faulty goods returned by customers are donated to charity wherever possible for resale on the second hand market rather than sent to landfill. The company also works closely with suppliers to ensure that all materials are sourced using sustainable methods and staff are paid a fair wage and have good working conditions.

SWOT Analysis

Joshua Edeki (Finance Director) has prepared the following SWOT analysis to evaluate Ruby Dale Ltd's competitive position:

Strengths

- Talented design team

- Dedicated management with lots of experience of working in the fashion goods sector

- Strong relationships with both suppliers and customers

- Globally recognised brand

Weaknesses

- Limit reached on current in-house manufacturing capacity

- Diseconomies of scale arising as a consequence of the larger workforce, for example communication issues, loss of co-ordination and low staff motivation

- Internal control weaknesses as a result of controls not evolving in step with the growing business

- Risk of overtrading

Opportunities

- Diversify further the product range, for example into eyewear, fragrance, watches and jewellery

- Open new shops to achieve a greater high street presence, for example in the growing markets of Asia and the emerging economies

- Outsource production to overseas manufacturers

- Float on the stock market to obtain additional finance to fund investment

Threats

- Downturn in the macro-economic environment which would impact upon the demand for luxury products

- Rise in the cost of materials

- Aggressive competitive action taken by other companies in the luxury goods sector in respect of poaching customers and obtaining prime retail sites

- Adverse market reaction to new product lines

Staff

Some of Ruby Dale Ltd's key personnel are listed below:

Managing Director	Ruby Dale
Entrepreneur and shareholder	Jack Carey
Finance Director	Joshua Edeki
Production Director	Mark Austin
Sales Director	Nadia Bibi
Financial Controller	Erika Tordoff
Purchasing Manager	Sophie Proud
Warehouse Manager	Ethan Box
Credit Controller	Abdul Rahman
Accounts Payable Clerk	Ella Maggs
Accounts Receivable Clerk	Luke Sinclair
General Accounts Clerk and Cashier	Alfred Tait
Payroll Clerk	Zoe Senior

Ruby Dale Ltd's financial statements

The financial statements of Ruby Dale Ltd – for the year ended 30 September 20X5 – show that the company had a turnover of £41.4 million, and made a profit after tax of £4.7 million.

Ruby Dale Ltd – Statement of profit or loss for the year ended 30 September 20X5

Operating statement	£000
Revenue	41,380
Cost of sales	(15,434)
Gross profit	25,946
Distribution costs	(11,428)
Administrative expenses	(7,160)
Profit from operations	7,358
Finance costs	(1,420)
Profit before tax	5,938
Tax	(1,260)
Profit for the period from continuing operations	4,678

Ruby Dale Ltd – Statement of financial position as at 30 September 20X5

	£000
ASSETS	
Non-current assets	
Property, plant and equipment	52,180
Current assets	
Inventories	3,780
Trade receivables	4,762
Cash and cash equivalents	676
	9,218
Total assets	61,398
EQUITY AND LIABILITIES	
Equity	
Ordinary share capital (£1 shares)	20,000
Retained earnings	16,836
Total equity	36,836
Non-current liabilities	
Bank loans	20,286
Current liabilities	
Trade payables	3,150
Tax liabilities	1,126
	4,276
Total liabilities	24,562
Total equity and liabilities	61,398

Synoptic assessment
Analysis of scenario: Ruby Dale Ltd

For assessments starting September 2019, AAT have issued a new live pre-release scenario, Ruby Dale Ltd (www.aat.org.uk/training/study-support/search).

It is essential that you have reviewed this prior to sitting your assessment. The synoptic assessment is designed to test your knowledge and application skills, and pull them together to demonstrate strong problem solving techniques.

Here is a summary of some of the key points from the pre-release information. This is not an exhaustive analysis, and there are areas which would benefit from further review and investigation.

You will be given narratives as well as financial information during the assessment in addition to the pre-release information. This is not available before the assessment, so be prepared to use this additional resource and adapt your answers accordingly.

If possible, investigate the financial statements of similar companies in the board games, toy cars and toy trains sector. You can then see whether the ratios and metrics from Ruby Dale Ltd appear reasonable.

A word on ratios: Ratios should be commented on, not just calculated and stated. If the information is available, compare it to previous years or to competitors' results. Consider what the ratio is telling you. If you are asked to discuss or explain or conclude information from a ratio, ensure you have given a justification for the movement (provided it is sensible and supported by facts, you will gain credit).

Key information provided

Please note that this information is not exhaustive and will give you a start on your pre-assessment analysis of the scenario.

Inventory

Inventory levels	High levels of inventory (20X5: 41% of current assets figure). Fashion retail business, with online and high street presence. Mix of products, with recent entry into new products including men's shoes.
Monitoring of inventory and product lines	Fashion is a fast moving industry and with the introduction of new product lines, there may be inventory which doesn't sell as well (untested new areas for the company, such as menswear). Consider the impact of cost versus net realisable value (IAS 2 *Inventories*). As there have been times when stock has sold out, leading to customers having unfulfilled sales, it is possible that Ruby Dale Ltd needs to analyse their faster moving product lines, and consider either a 'just in time' approach or review the inventory control system for these products.
Key ratios	**Breakeven point** $$BEP = \frac{Fixed\ costs}{Contribution\ per\ unit}$$ **Contribution/Sales ratio (CS ratio)** $$C/S\ ratio = \frac{Contribution}{Sales}$$ **Required profit calculations** $$\frac{Fixed\ costs + Required\ profit}{Contribution/unit}$$ **Margin of safety** $$\frac{Budgeted\ SV - Breakeven\ SV}{Budgeted\ SV} \times 100$$

Sales and trade receivables

Sales	The business has three main revenue streams: • Wholesale to major high street retailers and independent shops • Online retail business • Shop retail business (London, Paris, New York) Shop based retail • Expensive, premium locations. Possible issues with high business rates, long tenancy periods for the leaseholds of the shops (although the business may own the shops, it is unlikely, but no evidence given in the scenario) • 29 employees work in these shops. • Costs to cover prior to making a profit in these shops • Can control the environment and the 'look' that the company is aiming to achieve. • Customers can view the luxury products in premium surroundings • Possible opportunity for personal shoppers or VIP shopping experiences • Possible opportunity to have products bespoke to that location (for example, a New York handbag which can only be bought in that store, to draw customers to the stores). Especially if they cannot be purchased online. Online retail • Accessible to most customers, regardless of location • Can control the environment and the 'look' that the company is aiming to achieve. Wholesale to other stores • Potentially 'easier' cash flow (notwithstanding the current high street problems) as large inventory can be turned into cash, albeit at a lower sales margin. • Potential issues with security of credit terms to retail outlets • Debt factoring a consideration to enable cash quickly, albeit reducing the profit margin.

	These may each have differing sales margins, with direct online sales being the most profitable (in theory).
	Ruby Dale Ltd should look at what sales margins they are achieving, and also consider the cash flow impact of each: Although retail sales will offer better profit margins, the cash flow is likely to be lower, whereas the wholesale business to larger stores could offer a more reliable cash flow, but only by offering bulk discounts which will reduce inventory levels and profit margins.
Trade receivables are high	The trade receivables are high (making up 52% of the current assets figure).
	The narrative does not mention any issues that Ruby Dale Ltd may have had regarding their collection, but this amount could be down to a number of issues.
	• Poor credit control
	• Poor controls over which customers are able to obtain credit terms with Ruby Dale Ltd
	• A lack of review by management over the trade receivables
	• Uncertainty over recoverability of these receivables – there is no mention of an irrecoverable debt provision, so should there be one?
	• There could be an issue regarding the customer base – the scenario explains that they supply to major High Street retailers. Recently, there have been issues over large department stores (like House of Fraser and Debenhams) struggling for funding and being under pressure.

Staff and Directors

Experienced Management	Ruby is a talented creative person, but she has Jack who is an experienced entrepreneur.
Training	Opportunity to investigate further the training required by staff to boost morale, encourage staff retention and increase engagement with management. The company has 160 employees, so taking an average of £28,000 average salary, this brings the approximate annual salary charge to £4.48 million. As companies in the UK with a salary bill of over £3 million must contribute an apprenticeship levy of 0.5%, this means that Ruby Dale Ltd is contributing around £22,400 per annum. Ruby Dale Ltd should look to expand its apprenticeship programme to take advantage of the allowance per apprenticeship to offset the levy. Apprenticeships can be obtained in the creative industries, such as leather making, as well as business skills like team leader and software roles (potentially useful given the increasingly online nature of the retail sector). Apprentices will also remain with the business during their training, however, the company will have the apprenticeships attending college once a week in order for their 20% of training time to be accounted for.

Liquidity and investment

Potential stock market issue	Share capital is usually issued to finance capital investment or growth within the company. It is not primarily used to fund general working capital, so the company would need to ensure that they have specific plans for the financing from a listing, rather than just using it to fund general working capital.

You may be given further information, such as comparative data, whereby you can calculate ratios on liquidity to ascertain where the problems may lie.

By issuing new shares, this could dilute existing shareholdings potentially leading to issues with the current shareholders, Ruby and Jack. It is worth looking at the real life cases where entrepreneurs have listed on the stock exchange, only for them to lose their influence in the business and leave it, or those that have stayed on and thrived. |
| **Key ratios** | **Current ratio**

$$\frac{\text{Current assets}}{\text{Current liabilities}} = X:1$$

$$= \frac{3,780+4,762+676}{3,150+1,126}$$

= 2.2:1

Although the current liabilities of the business appear to easily cover the liabilities, this ratio does not consider the liquidity of inventory (refer to the quick ratio below) or any potential increase in capital (from a potential share issue) or potential new bank loan (both are longer term liabilities and so stating this ratio alone could be considered to be flawed).

Acid/Quick ratio

$$\frac{\text{Current assets} - \text{Inventories}}{\text{Current liabilities}} = X:1$$

$$\frac{4,762+676}{3,150+1,126} = \textbf{1.3: 1}$$

The quick ratio suggests that the ability for the business to 'cover' their current liabilities is reasonable, but once again, this is wholly dependent on the business collecting the trade receivables which make up the largest proportion |

of this figure. This ratio is limited by the elements of the current assets figure.

Gearing

$$\frac{\text{Non-current liabilities}}{\text{Total equity} + \text{Non-current liabilities}} \times 100 = X\%$$

$$\frac{20,286}{20,286 + 36,836} = 35\% \text{ gearing}$$

Gearing is concerned with the long-term financial stability of the company. It is looking at how much the company is financed by debt. The higher the gearing ratio, the less secure will be the financing of the company and possibly the company's future.

Ensure that you can compare the ratio or discuss it relevant to the scenario. Explain why the gearing ratio may be high, and what the issues may be (financing of debt, attractiveness to other investors, what is it funding exactly?). Also, a high gearing ratio in one industry may not be seen as risky as another, so having a look at industry standards for this type of business is another step you can take. Or compare it, if possible, to prior years or future plans in the real assessment.

Other ratios to calculate

Inventory turnover

$$\frac{\text{Cost of sales}}{\text{Inventories}}$$

Trade receivables collection period (debtor days)

$$\frac{\text{Trade receivables}}{\text{Revenue}} \times 365 \text{ days}$$

Trade payables payment period

$$\frac{\text{Trade payables}}{\text{Cost of sales}} \times 365 \text{ days}$$

Inventory holding period

$$\frac{\text{Inventory}}{\text{Cost of sales}} \times 365 \text{ days}$$

Environmental and sustainability

Environmental claims	The business has strong commitments to making their business as environmentally friendly and sustainable as possible.
	Points to note:
	• Donations of returned goods to charity (remember the Burberry scandal where they were found to be burning excess stock?)
	• Water saving and waste reduction efforts
Ethics	Ethical treatment of staff and suppliers is also high on their list. This is especially important when planning on outsourcing some of their manufacturing to Asia.
	Think about the impact on the brand if any adverse publicity is released or the financial impact of using fully audited companies in Asia. Ruby Dale Ltd is a British brand, how do their customers feel about taking the manufacturing overseas?

Overall analysis of the pre-release material

The scenario has provided a SWOT analysis.

You may be asked to use this information to provide a report to the Board of Directors discussing some of these elements.

Ensure that you are familiar with producing a variety of reports, including a balanced scorecard based on the SWOT analysis. You may also be asked to comment about some of the strengths, weaknesses, opportunities and threats identified.

Further steps

- Calculate ratios on the pre-release information as far as the information allows.

- Ensure you understand the benefits and issues with using certain ratios and can justify why you have used those particular ratios and not others.

- Review the financial statements of companies in the fashion sector, as this will broaden your knowledge and potentially highlight more issues which businesses in this sector can face, for example, Cath Kidston.

- AAT like to bring current issues in their Level 4 *Professional Diploma of Accounting Synoptic* assessment, so it is advisable to read financial papers, online news or look up financial statements on Companies House website. Some of these useful links will give you some material to start with.

- Please note that this list is not exhaustive and there may be elements for further discussion you have spotted or you think are relevant to the scenario.

Useful links

Cath Kidston Reports Annual Loss of 10.5 million pounds, (2019), Fashion United online at: //fashionunited.uk/news/business/cath-kidston-reports-annual-loss-of-10-5-million-pounds/2019011841085 [Accessed 15 May 2019]

Ruby Shoo set to expand its appeal with new casual styles to attract a wider customer base (2018), Drapers, available online at: https://www.drapersonline.com/product-and-trade-shows/brand-showcase/ruby-shoo-set-to-expand-its-appeal-with-new-casual-styles-to-attract-a-wider-customer-base/7029651.article [Accessed 15 May 2019]

Why Western fashion brands fail in China and tips on succeeding in a country where millennial consumers are taking over, South China Western Post (2018). Available online at: https://www.drapersonline.com/product-and-trade-shows/brand-showcase/ruby-shoo-set-to-expand-its-appeal-with-new-casual-styles-to-attract-a-wider-customer-base/7029651.article [Accessed 15 May 2019]

The 21 scariest data breaches of 2018 (2018), Business Insider, Available online at: https://www.businessinsider.com/data-hacks-breaches-biggest-of-2018-2018-12?r=US&IR=T [Accessed 15 May 2019]

Who's gone bust in retailing 2010-2019 (2019), Centre for Retail Research, Available online at: https://www.retailresearch.org/whosegonebust.php [Accessed 15 May 2019]

Superdry in profit warning ater heat wave hits sales (2018). BBC News, available online at https://www.bbc.co.uk/news/business-45860769 [Accessed 15 May 2019]

Employing an apprentice (2019), Gov.UK, available online at https://www.gov.uk/take-on-an-apprentice [Accessed 15 May 2019]

Two years in, is the apprenticeship levy still working? (2019) The Guardian, Available online at: www.theguardian.com/careers/2019/mar/05/two-years-in-is-the-apprenticeship-levy-still-working

What does Brexit mean for retailers? (2018) CMC Markets, available online at www.cmcmarkets.com/en-gb/news-and-analysis/what-does-brexit-mean-for-retail

UK retailers suffer weaker sales due to Brexit uncertainty (2019), The Guardian, available online at www.theguardian.com/business/2019/mar/05/uk-retailers-suffer-weaker-sales-due-to-brexit-uncertainty

Three quarters of entrepreneurs stay on after selling business (2018), Business Matters, Available online at: www.bmmagazine.co.uk/in-business/three-quarters-of-entrepreneurs-stay-on-after-selling-business/[Accessed 16 May 2019]

10 global companies that are environmentally friendly (2016), Virgin, available online at www.virgin.com/virgin-unite/10-global-companies-are-environmentally-friendly [Accessed 16 May 2019]

What is a sweatshop and do fashion brands still use them? (2019), Marie Clare Australia, Available online at www.marieclaire.com.au/sweat-shop [Accessed 16 May 2019]

BPP PRACTICE ASSESSMENT 1
LEVEL 4 SYNOPTIC ASSESSMENT

Time allowed: 3 hours

Level 4 Synoptic Assessment
BPP practice assessment 1

This practice assessment is based on the same scenario as AAT's sample assessment, SL Products Ltd. See pages 137–142 for the relevant pre-reading material.

....

Task 1 (20 marks)

(a) **Complete the following statement.**

The statutory duty to report whether SL Products Ltd's financial statements show a true and fair view is that of [▼] .

Picklist:

Companies House
Sue Hughes, the chief accountant
the company's directors
the company's auditors

At SL Products Ltd, the duties of processing purchase invoices, purchases ledger and processing payments are separated from each other. Tony Clark, purchasing manager, discovers that a goods returned note has not been followed up by a supplier's accounts department. No credit note has been received or posted to the purchases ledger.

(2 marks)

(b) **What is the correct action for Tony Clark to take?**

	✓
Prepare a journal to record the necessary reversal of the purchase invoice	
Prepare a debit note and send it to the supplier	
Advise the accounts payable clerk of the omission	
Advise Liz Hall, the accounts payable clerk, to reverse the relevant invoice from the purchases day book	

(2 marks)

(c) **Matthew Tunnock, the accounts receivable clerk, has asked you to show whether the following errors would be detected by reconciling the sales ledger to the sales ledger control account.**

VAT on a sales invoice posted to sales instead of VAT control	▼
A sales invoice credited to the customer's account	▼
A sales invoice posted to the wrong customer account	▼
A batch of purchase invoices posted to the sales ledger control account	▼
A pricing error in a sales invoice	▼

Picklist:

Would be detected
Would not be detected

(5 marks)

You have been asked to set up an 8-character password for SL Products Ltd's accounting system.

(d) **Which of the following would be the most secure?**

	✓
98765432	
acsystem	
1jan2000	
?win121#	

(2 marks)

Your duties at SL Products Ltd include running credit checks on new customers. Recently the company has offered a large credit limit to Howlsons Ltd. Its finance director has sent you the following email to thank you for your support:

'Thank you for helping us agree terms of trade with SL Products Ltd. Now that our two companies are connected in this way I trust you will share with me any information you have about BFA Ltd, who also buys from you and who is our biggest competitor.'

(e) Answer the following questions.

Which of your fundamental principles is threatened by this request?

▼

Picklist:

Confidentiality
Objectivity
Professional behaviour

What action should you take?

▼

Picklist:

You can share some information but must advise BFA Ltd
You must notify the National Crime Agency of the request
You must refuse to share any information

(4 marks)

Louise Harding, the Financial Director has asked you to look at the management accounts. She wants you to determine who will be performing the analysis and has asked you to classify the different types of information.

(f) Identify the type of information provided in the following management reports

Wastage reports from the production line	▼
Inventory turnover reports	▼
Inventory level reports	▼
Future demand estimates for the next 12 months	▼
Analysis of competitor's products and their market positioning	▼

Picklist:

Operational
Strategic
Tactical

(5 marks)

Task 2 (15 marks)

SL Products Ltd has a controlling interest in Merville Ltd. Unaudited accounts for Merville Ltd's financial year ended 31 December 20X3 have been prepared and an operating budget for 20X4 has been drafted for approval by the directors of SL Products Ltd.

You have been asked to review the budget submission by the directors of Merville Ltd.

Budget submission

Please find attached our budget proposal for 20X4. Actual (unaudited) results for 20X3 are provided for comparison. Your approval of the budget is requested.

Steady sales growth was achieved in 20X3. During the year we introduced five innovative new products which were quite well-received by the marketplace. All our products are patented in the UK and are therefore protected from direct competition in the UK.

In 20X4, Merville Ltd will continue selling to our own customers and through SL Products Ltd's catalogue. To achieve the targets set for us by our majority shareholder, SL Products Ltd, we also plan to set up and run our own website for selling our products and those of other manufacturers. We aim to start making a great many sales in the EU for the first time.

In total we have 55 products at different stages of their product life cycle. We are in the course of developing three new products. Although it is difficult to achieve raised prices for high-tech products once launched, we hope our new website and the extension of sales into Europe justify a budgeted rise in all our prices, as required by SL Products Ltd. We have therefore budgeted for 10% volume growth in all our products, and approximately 20% revenue growth.

A review of processes in 20X3 means we have been able to start operating more efficiently so we are budgeting for a 2% decrease in costs, again as required by SL Products Ltd.

Overall we are budgeting for a huge increase in the level of profits and the rate of profitability, as required by SL Products Ltd.

Product range at start of 20X3: 50. Product range at end of 20X3: 55. New products to be launched in 20X4: 3.

Operating budget for year ended 31 December 20X4	Unaudited results 20X3	Draft budget 20X4
Sales volume (units)	8,500	9,350
	£	£
Sales revenue	1,239,460	1,490,000
Costs:		
Materials	291,750	286,000
Labour	470,830	461,400
Production overheads	145,030	142,100
Depreciation	52,000	51,000
Marketing	19,500	19,100
Administration	105,420	103,300
Total	1,084,530	1,062,900
Operating profit	154,930	427,100
Operating profit % to sales	12.5%	28.7%

Prepare a report for the chief accountant of SL Products Ltd in three sections as follows:

(a) Examine the planning assumptions and calculations in the proposed budget and identify any weaknesses.

(5 marks)

(b) Evaluate how well the budget would motivate managers to create sustainable, profitable growth.

(5 marks)

(c) **Explain how using zero-based budgeting could assist the directors of Merville Ltd.**

(5 marks)

Task 3 (15 marks)

You have been asked to review the adequacy of the control in SL Products Ltd's sales procedures. Your review has established the following information.

The company operates an integrated accounting system which includes a sales accounting module. Cynthia Moss, the Sales Director, is responsible for managing sales activities.

Ordering and despatch:

- All sales, except those for cash, must be documented on an official customer order. The order should state the agreed price, if known.

- Customer orders must be reviewed and signed by Cynthia Moss.

- Large orders must be signed by Louise Harding, the Finance Director.

- Five copies of the customer order form are printed. Once signed, the original is sent to the customer as an acknowledgement. A copy printed on yellow paper is sent to Matthew Tunnock, the accounts receivable clerk. A pink copy is sent to production and a green copy is sent to despatch. The orange copy is retained by the individual who took the order.

- When the goods are completed, production signs the pink copy and sends it to despatch.

- When the goods are sent out, despatch signs the green copy and sends it, with the pink copy, to Matthew Tunnock.

New customers:

- New customers are contacted by Ray Massey, the Credit Controller. He asks for a trade reference and banking details, and offers credit terms.

- He usually offers payment terms as follows:

    - One month from the end of the month in which delivery takes place.
    - With a 5% discount for payment within 21 days of delivery.

    However, terms are subject to negotiation.

Accounting:

- All sales invoices are raised by Matthew Tunnock. He matches yellow, pink and green copy orders and prepares the invoices for sending to the customer.

- He posts the invoices to the computerised accounting system.

- He answers queries from customers, issuing credit notes when appropriate.

- Most customers pay by bank transfer. Matthew Tunnock checks the bank account weekly and posts receipts to the ledger accounts.

Complete your review as follows:

- **Identify FIVE systemic weaknesses in the company's internal controls for handling sales on credit.**

- **Explain how each weakness that you have identified could create a problem for the company.**

Note. You are **not** required to make recommendations to change procedures.

No.	Weakness	Potential problem

(15 marks)

Task 4 (15 marks)

Review of product pricing

SL Products Ltd has recently suffered a further decline in its gross profit margin. Cynthia Moss (Sales Director) and Louise Harding (Finance Director) are reviewing the situation so they can report to the Board of Directors with proposals to halt the decline.

The market for the company's high-tech products is very competitive, and success depends on constant innovation and better quality than competitor products. After about two years, a product enters the decline phase of its product life-cycle, when there is no scope for price increases and the likelihood of obsolete inventory.

Sue Hughes, the Chief Accountant, proposes that all new products should be priced to give a 25% margin on sales price, to generate as much profit as possible in the early years. She tells you there are two new products that are ready for launch: the AB, the CD and the EF.

The company uses a full overhead recovery pricing model. Variable production overheads are equal to 20% of materials and labour, which are all variable.

(a) **Complete the calculation of the proposed selling prices based on a 25% margin.**

Prices for new products	£ per unit	
	AB	CD
Materials and labour	72.00	45.00
Variable production overheads		
Fixed production overheads	6.00	3.00
Other fixed overheads	6.30	3.60
Total cost		
Price at 25% margin		

(4 marks)

Cynthia Moss, the sales director, says that Sue's approach to pricing may not be competitive. She has compared each of the two products (AB and CD) with competitors' products and has estimated the sales potential at three price levels; one at the price you calculated in (a), one which is designed to be cheaper than competitor prices, and one at market price.

Price levels and estimated annual volumes	AB		CD	
	£ each	Volume	£ each	Volume
Price at 25% margin	See (a)	175	See (a)	250
Cheaper than competitor price	125.00	300	65.00	500
Market price	130.00	275	75.00	300

Cynthia wants you to calculate which prices would be most profitable.

(b) **For each product, calculate the marginal cost per unit and the annual contribution that would be earned based on each price and volume.**

	AB £	CD £
Marginal cost per unit		
Annual contribution if price level is...		
...price at 25% margin		
...cheaper than competitor price		
...market price		

(8 marks)

(c) **Would the proposed policy of pricing at 25% margin ensure that all new products at least break even? (You can assume that the costs are correctly calculated.)**

▼

Picklist:

Yes

No

(1 mark)

(d) Explain your answer to (c).

(2 marks)

Task 5 (20 marks)

Louise Harding, the Finance Director, is preparing a presentation for the Board of Directors. She has asked you to complete a comparative 'score card' of key financial ratios which she will use as part of her presentation.

Relevant data has been extracted from the last two years' accounts. These extracts do not include the results of Merville Ltd.

Extracts from accounts of SL Products Ltd	Year ended 31 December 20X2 £000	Year ended 31 December 20X3 £000
Sales revenue	20,900	21,200
Cost of sales	15,144	15,609
Profit from operations	470	328
Assets		
Non-current assets	4,234	3,701
Inventories	3,908	4,579
Trade receivables	3,032	3,384
Cash and equivalents	6	8
Total	**11,180**	**11,672**
Equity and Liabilities		
Equity	5,550	5,600
Non-current liabilities	1,400	1,600
Trade payables	3,730	4,020
Bank overdraft	260	302
Tax liabilities	240	150
Total	**11,180**	**11,672**

(a) **Complete the scorecard by calculating the missing ratios.**

SL Products Ltd Scorecard	Year ended 31 Dec 20X2	Year ended 31 Dec 20X3
Profitability and gearing (correct to 1 dp):		
Gross profit %	27.5 %	_____ %
Operating profit %	2.2 %	_____ %
Return on capital employed	6.8 %	_____ %
Gearing	20.1 %	_____ %
Liquidity ratios (correct to 1 dp):		
Current ratio	1.6:1	_____ :1
Acid test/quick ratio	0.7:1	_____ :1
Working capital days (correct to nearest day):		
Inventory holding period	94 days	_____ days
Trade receivables collection period	53 days	_____ days
Trade payables payment period	90 days	_____ days
Working capital cycle	57 days	_____ days

(10 marks)

(b) **Select the ONE correct observation about each aspect of business performance below.**

Profitability

	✓
Profitability has dipped slightly, due to poor sales.	
The profitability ratios give serious cause for concern. The small increase in sales revenue has failed to compensate for increased cost of sales and operating expenses.	

	✓
The ratios give mixed messages. Some have improved and some have deteriorated. Further investigation is required.	

(2 marks)

Gearing

	✓
The increased gearing ratio only reflects the fact that an extra loan has been taken out.	
The increased gearing ratio shows that equity has increased at a greater rate than non-current liabilities.	
The increased gearing ratio shows that the company has become more risky.	

(2 marks)

Liquidity

	✓
Both ratios have deteriorated which indicates that the company is less solvent.	
Both ratios have improved, indicating there are no concerns about the company's liquidity or solvency.	
The improvement in the liquidity ratios indicates that the company is succeeding in managing its cash flows.	

(2 marks)

Working capital

	✓
The longer working capital cycle indicates the company is insolvent.	
The shorter working capital cycle indicates the company can repay some of its long-term liabilities.	
The change in the working capital cycle requires urgent investigation.	

(2 marks)

Overall performance

	✓
Profitability has declined in 20X3, mainly due to competitive pressures. However, the gearing and liquidity measures show an improving financial position.	
20X3 has been a bad year. Profitability has declined and finances are coming under serious pressure.	
Steady progress has been made in 20X3. The ratios show that the company is being better managed.	

(2 marks)

Task 6 (15 marks)

You have been asked to carry out a review of SL Products Ltd's purchases order processing procedure and make recommendations for improvement.

You have interviewed the Finance Director (Louise Harding), the Production Director (Colin Smith) and the Purchasing Manager (Tony Clark). Your findings are below.

- Suppliers are identified and contacted direct by individuals who require the goods or service in question.

- All purchases on credit are recorded on an official purchase order by that individual. The order states the price and delivery date, if known.

- All departments are provided with books of pre-numbered order forms. These books can be obtained from the stationery store.

- Capital expenditure orders must be raised and signed by Louise Harding.

- Other orders must be signed by the individual placing the order.

- New suppliers are given a trade reference and banking details by Tony Clark, who also requests credit terms. These are subject to negotiation, though the company's preferred terms are to pay 60 days from the end of the month in which delivery takes place.

You are required to identify four features of these procedures: one strength; one weakness; one threat and one opportunity. Do not use the same feature more than once.

(a) **Identify a strength in these procedures. Explain how the business benefits from the strength.**

(3 marks)

(b) **Identify a weakness in these procedures. Explain how the weakness damages the business and suggest a remedy.**

(4 marks)

(c)   Identify an opportunity to improve the procedures to the benefit of the business.

(4 marks)

(d)   Identify a threat in these procedures that could damage the business and suggest an action that would reduce the risk.

(4 marks)

BPP PRACTICE ASSESSMENT 1
LEVEL 4 SYNOPTIC ASSESSMENT

ANSWERS

Level 4 Synoptic Assessment
BPP practice assessment 1: answers

Task 1 (20 marks)

(a) The statutory duty to report whether SL Products Ltd's financial statements show a true and fair view is that of the company's auditors .

(2 marks)

(b)

	✓
Prepare a journal to record the necessary reversal of the purchase invoice	
Prepare a debit note and send it to the supplier	
Advise the Accounts Payable Clerk of the omission	✓
Advise Liz Hall, the Accounts Payable Clerk, to reverse the relevant invoice from the purchases day book	

(2 marks)

(c)

VAT on a sales invoice posted to sales instead of VAT control	Would not be detected
A sales invoice credited to the customer's account	Would be detected
A sales invoice posted to the wrong customer account	Would not be detected
A batch of purchase invoices posted to the sales ledger control account	Would be detected
A pricing error in a sales invoice	Would not be detected

(5 marks)

(d)

	✓
98765432	
acsystem	
1jan2000	
?win121#	✓

(2 marks)

(e)

Confidentiality

You must refuse to share any information

(4 marks)

(f)

Wastage reports from the production line	Operational
Inventory turnover reports	Tactical
Inventory level reports	Operational
Future demand estimates for the next 12 months	Strategic
Analysis of competitor's products and their market positioning	Strategic

(5 marks)

Task 2 (15 marks)

(a)

The draft budget for 20X4 is based on the assumption of 10% growth in sales volume and 20% growth in revenue, despite a decrease of 2% across the board in costs. This appears to be a very ambitious plan which the directors say is justified by the company's expansion into the EU and by the new website. I suggest that we need to:

- Review the market in the EU, which will be much more competitive than the UK as patent protection for the company's products does not extend beyond the UK

- Review the assumptions about the website, in which the company appears to have no experience and for which it does not appear to have budgeted any additional costs (these would appear under Marketing, which shows the same 2% decrease as all other cost categories)

- Review the reasons for the company's declining rate of product innovation (five new products launched in 20X3; only three planned in 20X4) and how the ageing product portfolio affects the growth projection for 20X4

All costs have been decreased by 2% in the draft budget. This takes no account of the volume growth nor the effects of inflation. While it is positive that the review of processes shows scope for efficiency, it seems unlikely that all variable and fixed costs would show the same scope for decrease. In particular, I would expect to see increased marketing spend because of the website and expansion into Europe. Each line of costs needs to be considered carefully according to its cost type (variable, fixed, etc) and its own cost pressures.

(5 marks)

(b)

The budget does not seem to be realistic. This appears to be because SL Products Ltd has given the directors of Merville Ltd targets for volume and revenue growth, and cost decreases, without involvement in how they can be achieved. Merville Ltd has simply translated these targets into the budget without serious consideration of whether they are realistic or achievable.

Budgetary control can be a powerful tool to encourage managers and staff to create sustainable, profitable growth. To do this, budgets need to be stretching but still achievable.

As the projections for revenue and costs cannot really be achieved they will not help the company either to plan or control its operations in the year ahead. Managers at Merville Ltd will be demotivated by having targets imposed on them which have not been thought through. They will not have 'ownership' of the figures and therefore will not be motivated to achieve them.

I do not believe that this draft budget would motivate Merville Ltd to create sustainable, profitable growth.

(5 marks)

(c)

> Merville Ltd's directors could use zero-based budgeting to review each product and each line of cost in its operations from scratch. This will determine what is realistically achievable for the year ahead. It may be that some costs will no longer be required at all, as suggested by the efficiency review that has already taken place. It might also be that some products will be able to achieve a price rise and volume increases, but not all.
>
> Zero-based budgeting can be a powerful tool for a company to plan and control its operations better in future, though it can be a costly and time-consuming process.

(5 marks)

Task 3 (15 marks)

Marking guide: A maximum of 5 weaknesses and the potential problems, with each weakness awarded 1 mark and each problem 2 marks (to a maximum of 3 marks).

No.	Weakness	Potential problem
1	Cynthia Moss appears to have very little involvement in day to day sales, apart from negotiating terms with new customers.	Failures in the system and system abuses could go unnoticed.
2	The procedures do not include any mention of checking that goods of the correct category and standard have been despatched.	If this is not happening the company could be sending out sub-standard goods.
3	Orders can be taken without agreeing a price.	The company is in a weak position to negotiate price after the goods or service have been despatched.
4	Lack of authorisation of new accounts.	There should be a policy for deciding on whether to offer credit at all. Potential for fraud through collusion with customers.
5	The terms agreed by Ray Massey are not countersigned.	Potential for fraud through collusion with customers.
6	Only one signature is required on most orders.	Potential for fraud through collusion with customers.

No.	Weakness	Potential problem
7	Matthew Tunnock checks, clears and arranges payment of invoices.	Potential for fraud through collusion with customers.
8	Matthew Tunnock controls all aspects of sales accounting.	Potential for fraud.
9	Receipts are only monitored and posted once a week.	Increases the opportunity for teeming and lading, and means a bad service will be given to customers if they ring with a query.
10	No counter-signatory required for credit notes.	Potential for fraud through collusion with customers.

(15 marks)

Note. Only **five** weaknesses were required.

Task 4 (15 marks)

(a)

Prices for new products	£ per unit	
	AB	**CD**
Materials and labour	72.00	45.00
Variable production overheads (W1)	14.40	9.00
Fixed production overheads	6.00	3.00
Other fixed overheads	6.30	3.60
Total cost	98.70	60.60
Price at 25% margin (W2)	131.60	80.80

Workings

(1) 20% × materials and labour
(2) Total cost ÷ 0.75

(4 marks)

(b)

	AB £	CD £
Marginal cost per unit	86.40	54.00
Annual contribution if price level is...		
...price at 25% margin	7,910	6,700
...cheaper than competitor price	11,580	5,500
...market price	11,990	6,300

(8 marks)

(c)

Yes

(1 mark)

(d)

The 25% margin prices are based on full cost because the company operates a full overhead recovery pricing model. This means that, at the 25% margin price, each product breaks even by covering its fixed costs, then makes a positive contribution to profit.

(2 marks)

Task 5 (20 marks)

(a)

SL Products Ltd Scorecard	Year ended 31 Dec 20X2	Year ended 31 Dec 20X3
Profitability and gearing (correct to 1 dp):		
Gross profit %	27.5%	26.4 %
Operating profit %	2.2%	1.5 %
Return on capital employed	6.8%	4.6 %
Gearing	20.1%	22.2 %

SL Products Ltd Scorecard	Year ended 31 Dec 20X2	Year ended 31 Dec 20X3
Liquidity ratios (correct to 1 dp):		
Current ratio	1.6:1	1.8 :1
Acid test/quick ratio	0.7:1	0.8 :1
Working capital days (correct to nearest day):		
Inventory holding period	94 days	107 days
Trade receivables collection period	53 days	58 days
Trade payables payment period	90 days	94 days
Working capital cycle	57 days	71 days

(10 marks)

(b)   Profitability

	✓
Profitability has dipped slightly, due to poor sales.	
The profitability ratios give serious cause for concern. The small increase in sales revenue has failed to compensate for increased cost of sales and operating expenses.	✓
The ratios give mixed messages. Some have improved and some have deteriorated. Further investigation is required.	

(2 marks)

Gearing

	✓
The increased gearing ratio only reflects the fact that an extra loan has been taken out.	
The increased gearing ratio shows that equity has increased at a greater rate than non current liabilities.	
The increased gearing ratio shows that the company has become more risky.	✓

(2 marks)

Liquidity

	✓
Both ratios have deteriorated which indicates that the company is less solvent.	
Both ratios have improved, indicating there are no concerns about the company's liquidity or solvency.	
The improvement in the liquidity ratios indicates that the company is succeeding in managing its cash flows.	✓

(2 marks)

Working capital

	✓
The longer working capital cycle indicates the company is insolvent.	
The shorter working capital cycle indicates the company can repay some of its long-term liabilities.	
The change in the working capital cycle requires urgent investigation.	✓

(2 marks)

Overall performance

	✓
Profitability has declined in 20X3, mainly due to competitive pressures. However, the gearing and liquidity measures show an improving financial position.	
20X3 has been a bad year. Profitability has declined and finances are coming under serious pressure.	✓
Steady progress has been made in 20X3. The ratios show that the company is being better managed.	

(2 marks)

Task 6 (15 marks)

Tutorial note. The question only requires one strength and one weakness. Additional items are provided here to illustrate the range of possible answers.

(a)

> **(i)** The highest value items – for capital expenditure – require senior management authority before being ordered, and all purchases on credit require proper purchase orders. Staff understand therefore that proper procedures must be followed before items can be purchased, which reduces the risk of unnecessary items being bought by the company or that staff purchase items for themselves at the company's expense.
>
> **(ii)** A coherent approach is taken towards negotiating credit terms with suppliers, which benefits the company's cash flow and planning.

(3 marks)

(b)

> **(i)** It appears items can be purchased from suppliers without a price or delivery time having been agreed upon. This introduces unnecessary uncertainty into the company's operations, costs and cash flows. The remedy is that no purchase orders may be raised without an agreed price being stated on them.
>
> **(ii)** There is no security over the purchase order forms, so in theory any staff member or other person may obtain a form and purchase items to the account of SL Products Ltd. This means the company may be liable to pay for items it has not received or does not want. The remedy is to ensure that purchases can only be recorded and paid for if the purchase invoice when received can be matched to a purchase order.
>
> **(iii)** Outside of capital expenditure there is no need for countersignature to indicate higher authority, and no cash limit on an individual purchase. In theory this could result in large amounts being spent inappropriately.

(4 marks)

(c)

> The involvement of Tony Clark, the Purchasing Manager, with suppliers seems to focus only on how long the company can take to pay. There is an opportunity to expand his role significantly to: (1) identify and quality assure suppliers independently of user departments; (2) guide and authorise departments in their purchases; and (3) negotiate prices, delivery terms and discounts with existing and new suppliers.

(4 marks)

(d)

> The lack of supervision and co-ordination of purchasing suggests that optimum purchasing quantities and careful inventory management are completely overlooked. This could leave the company with significant amounts of inventory that it does not need and cannot use. As well as making a loss on these items, the business will also suffer cash flow problems. There is an urgent need for a more coherent approach to purchasing, especially but not only for Production, so that the company achieves a balance between having inventory when it is needed and having too high a level that drains its resources.

(4 marks)

BPP PRACTICE ASSESSMENT 2
LEVEL 4 SYNOPTIC ASSESSMENT

Time allowed: 3 hours

Level 4 Synoptic Assessment
BPP practice assessment 2

This practice assessment is based on the same scenario as AAT's sample assessment, SL Products Ltd. See pages 127–131 for the relevant pre-reading material.

Task 1 (20 marks)

(a) Complete the following statement.

The statutory duty to maintain a public record of information about SL Products Ltd is that of [▾] .

Picklist:

Companies House
Sue Hughes, the chief accountant
the company's directors
the company's auditors

At SL Products Ltd the task of preparing the payroll is performed by Jane Patel, Payroll Clerk. Within the company line managers authorise staff timesheets, and Hina Khan (General Accounts Clerk and cashier) processes payments to employees. Colin Smith, Production Director, discovers that the timesheet of the production supervisor, Naseem Hadid, has been omitted from the weekly payroll.

(2 marks)

(b) What is the correct action for Colin Smith to take?

	✓
Instruct Hina Khan to make an immediate bank transfer to Naseem	
Advise Jane Patel of the omission	
Prepare a journal to record Naseem's gross pay	
Write out a cheque for Naseem	

(2 marks)

(c)   **Jane Patel, the Payroll Clerk, has asked you to show whether the following errors would be detected by clearing the wages control account.**

Ten hours pay paid to J. Utley instead of T. Utley	▾
Gross pay credited to an expense account	▾
Payment of PAYE to the pension administrator rather than HMRC	▾
Miscalculation of employer's National Insurance	▾
A transposition error in the net pay authority given to BACS	▾

Picklist:

Would be detected
Would not be detected

(5 marks)

You have been asked to ensure the correct controls are in place to validate data input to SL Products Ltd's accounting system.

(d)   **Which of the following types of control are relevant?**

	✔
System controls	
Physical access controls	
Integrity controls	

(2 marks)

Your duties at SL Products Ltd include preparing the consolidated accounts. Sue Hughes, the chief accountant, is aware that the company's most recent results are not good. She has instructed you to ensure that, when valuing inventory, the highest possible valuation is placed on each item whether or not this is in line with IAS 2 *Inventories*.

(e) **Answer the following questions.**

Which of your fundamental principles is threatened by this request?

▼

Picklist:

Confidentiality
Integrity
Objectivity

What action should you take?

▼

Picklist:

You must comply with IAS 2 *Inventories*
You must comply with Sue's instruction
You must notify the National Crime Agency of Sue's instruction

(4 marks)

(f) **Identify whether each of the following control activities is an integrity, system, physical access or management security control. Select your answer using the picklist (answers may be used more than once).**

Keypad entry to the accounting office	▼
User access restrictions to areas of the accountancy software	▼
Review of the log file for access of areas of the accountancy system by the Financial Director	▼

Picklist:

Integrity control
Physical access control
System control

(3 marks)

(g) **Which TWO of the following statements reflects a tall organisational structure**

	✓
Management have a wide span of control	
Structure is highly dependent on hierarchy	
Management do a wide variety of tasks within the organisation	
Management have a smaller team, with clear, strict boundaries and tasks set	

(2 marks)

Task 2 (15 marks)

Cynthia Moss, Sales Director, has performed a review of the products sold by the newly acquired subsidiary Merville Ltd. She has discovered that three products sold are similar. Details of the selling prices and costs of these products are as follows:

	Product XC72 £	Product FH54 £	Product GG44 £
Selling price per unit	245	225	230
Variable costs per unit			
Materials	120	110	70
Labour (@£15/hour)	30	22.50	45
Allocated fixed overheads per unit	25	30	50
Total cost per unit	190	162.50	165
Profit per unit	70	62.50	65

Cynthia has suggested that Merville should discontinue production of FH54 and GG44 and only produce and sell XC72, as this generates the most profit per unit.

(a) **Critically evaluate this strategy**

(7 marks)

(b) **Discuss the impact on your answer if you discover that each of these three products requires the same specialist labour and that it is likely to be in short supply over the next two years.**

(8 marks)

Task 3 (15 marks)

(a) You have found a number of systemic weaknesses in the internal controls in SL Products Ltd's accounting system. Identify what, if any, effect each one will have on the company's reported profit.

Systemic weakness	No effect on reported profit ✓	Understatement of reported profit ✓	Overstatement of reported profit ✓
Omitting sales			
Understating the allowance for doubtful debts			
Overstating assets			
Understating expenses			
Writing off valid debts as irrecoverable			
Undervaluation of inventory at the period end			

(6 marks)

You have been asked to review the adequacy of the control in SL Products Ltd's payroll procedures. Your review has established the following information.

The company operates an integrated accounting system which includes a payroll accounting module. Sue Hughes, the Chief Accountant, is responsible for managing payroll activities. Jane Patel, the Payroll Clerk, performs day-to-day payroll tasks.

Jane Patel's responsibilities include:

- Maintaining standing data on employees
- Recording each employee's hours at work where this information is relevant and available
- Calculating gross pay and deductions
- Preparing the wages control account

- Preparing the BACS payments each month to employees and HMRC
- Reconciling total pay and deductions in the wages control account

Once a month, after the payroll and its associated payments are complete, Sue Hughes reviews total payroll cost against budget and investigates unexpected variances.

(b) **Which THREE of the following types of control activity are weakest in SL Products Ltd's payroll system?**

	✓
Physical controls	
Segregation of duties	
Management controls	
Supervisory controls	
Organisation	
Authorisation (approval) of transactions	
Arithmetic and bookkeeping checks	
Personnel controls	

(3 marks)

(c) **Explain THREE ways in which the weak control activities could create problems for the company.**

Note. You are **not** required to make recommendations to change procedures.

(i)

(ii)

(iii)

(6 marks)

Task 4 (15 marks)

You have been given the following information for the manufacture of units of HW by SL Products Ltd for the month just ended.

	Budget		Actual	
Production (units of HW)		48,000		50,400
Direct materials	19,200 kg	£230,400	20,600 kg	£252,350

Louise Harding, the Finance Director, has asked you to write a note to help in the training of a junior accounting technician. The notes are to explain the calculation of the total direct material variance and how this variance can be split into a price variance and a usage variance.

(a) **Explain the total direct material variance and how it can be split into a price variance and usage variance. Use calculations to illustrate your explanation.**

(10 marks)

Sue Hughes, the Chief Accountant, has prepared the following budgetary control report for the product QR produced by SL Products Ltd, together with the variances calculated below.

	Budget		Actual	
Production (units)		5,100		5,500
Direct materials	15,500 kg	£57,320	15,600 kg	£54,600
Direct labour	10,200 hours	£112,200	12,100 hours	£139,150
Fixed overheads		£97,500		£96,300
Total cost		£267,020		£290,050

Variances	Amount £
Direct materials price	3,090 F
Direct materials usage	4,130 F
Direct labour rate	6,050 A
Direct labour efficiency	Not yet calculated
Fixed overhead expenditure	Not yet calculated

SL Products Ltd normally prepares an operating statement under standard absorption costing principles but Louise Harding, the Finance Director, has asked you to prepare an operating statement under standard marginal costing principles.

(b) Place each variance into the correct column (favourable or adverse) and complete the table.

			£
Budgeted variable cost for actual production			
Budgeted fixed cost			
Total budgeted cost for actual production			
Variance	**Favourable £**	**Adverse £**	
Direct materials price			
Direct materials usage	4,130		
Direct labour rate			
Direct labour efficiency			
Fixed overhead expenditure			
Fixed overhead volume			
Total variance			9,730
Actual cost of actual production			

(5 marks)

Task 5 (20 marks)

Louise Harding, the Finance Director, is preparing a presentation for the Board of Directors. She has asked you to complete a comparative 'score card' of key financial ratios which she will use as part of her presentation.

Relevant data has been extracted from the last two years' accounts. These extracts do not include the results of Merville Ltd.

Extracts from accounts of SL Products Ltd	Year ended 31 December 20X3 £000	Year ended 31 December 20X4 £000
Sales revenue	21,200	23,900
Cost of sales	15,609	15,904
Profit from operations	328	508
Assets		
Non-current assets	3,701	4,715
Inventories	4,579	3,197
Trade receivables	3,384	2,559
Cash and equivalents	8	38
Total	**11,672**	**10,509**
Equity and Liabilities		
Equity	5,600	6,200
Non-current liabilities	1,600	1,000
Trade payables	4,020	3,099
Bank overdraft	302	0
Tax liabilities	150	210
Total	**11,672**	**10,509**

(a) Complete the scorecard by calculating the missing ratios for the year ended 31 December 20X4.

SL Products Ltd Scorecard	Year ended 31 Dec 20X3	Year ended 31 Dec 20X4
Profitability and gearing (correct to 1 dp):		
Gross profit %	26.4%	☐ %
Operating profit %	1.5%	☐ %
Return on capital employed	4.6%	☐ %
Gearing	22.2%	☐ %
Liquidity ratios (correct to 1 dp):		
Current ratio	1.8:1	☐ :1
Acid test/quick ratio	0.8:1	☐ :1
Working capital days (correct to nearest day):		
Inventory holding period	107 days	☐ days
Trade receivables collection period	58 days	☐ days
Trade payables payment period	94 days	☐ days
Working capital cycle	71 days	☐ days

(10 marks)

(b) Select the **ONE** correct observation about each aspect of business performance below.

Profitability

	✓
Profitability has improved due to improved sales and reduced costs.	
The profitability ratios have improved due to increased sales, but cost control is still a problem.	

	✓
The ratios give mixed messages. Some have improved and some have deteriorated. Further investigation is required.	

(2 marks)

Gearing

	✓
The reduced gearing ratio reflects that equity has partially replaced lending in the company's financial structure.	
The level of gearing is not related to the company's profitability.	
The increased gearing ratio shows that the company has become more risky.	

(2 marks)

Liquidity

	✓
Both ratios have deteriorated which indicates that the company is less solvent.	
Both ratios have improved, indicating there are no concerns about the company's liquidity or solvency.	
Comparing the liquidity ratios with last year's tells us little about the company's solvency.	

(2 marks)

Working capital

	✓
The longer working capital cycle indicates the company is insolvent.	
The shorter working capital cycle indicates the company has addressed some solvency issues that appeared in 20X3.	
The change in the working capital cycle requires urgent investigation.	

(2 marks)

Overall performance and position

	✓
The company has a new shareholder whose cash has been used to invest in improving profitability and reducing financial risk.	
Steady progress has been made in 20X4, but profitability has declined and the company remains risky.	
The company continues to perform badly and is in danger of insolvency	

(2 marks)

Task 6 (15 marks)

In the last year SL Products Ltd's subsidiary, Merville Ltd, has found serious weaknesses in each of its three main transaction streams which arise from particular uncontrolled risks. Its finance director has asked you for advice on how to avoid or reduce these risks.

(a) **You are required to identify ONE control objective and ONE control activity for each risk.**

Transaction stream	Risk	Control objective	Control activity
Payroll	Company is fined for non-compliance with PAYE regulations		
Sales	Company charges for goods in error and loses custom		
Purchasing	Company pays more than once for the same goods and the supplier does not correct the mistake		

(6 marks)

Sue Hughes, the Chief Accountant, presents you with Merville Ltd's monthly operating report. The original budget has been flexed to the level of actual activity, and variances calculated.

You are told that:

* Material, labour and distribution costs are variable.

* Power is a semi-variable cost. The fixed element is budgeted at £5,300 per month.

* Premises costs are stepped, budgeted to double at every 75,000 units of monthly production (at this level the company hires a second workshop at a daily all-inclusive rate).

* Depreciation, marketing and administration costs are fixed.

* The company does not use full absorption costing.

Monthly operating report

Original budget		Flexed budget	Actual	Variance Fav/(Adv)
74,200	Sales volume (units)		80,000	
£		£	£	£
534,240	Sales revenue	576,000	581,400	5,400
	Costs			
192,920	Materials	208,000	211,520	–3,520
200,340	Labour	216,000	221,300	–5,300
29,680	Distribution	32,000	33,100	–1,100
27,560	Power	29,300	29,150	150
10,000	Premises costs	20,000	10,000	10,000
3,650	Depreciation	3,650	3,600	50
32,500	Marketing	32,500	33,400	–900
10,670	Administration	10,670	9,980	690
507,320	Total	552,120	552,050	70
26,920	Operating profit/(loss)	23,880	29,350	5,470

Write an email to Sue Hughes to explain:

(b)   The main factors that led to the actual profit being higher than the original budgeted profit.

(5 marks)

(c)   How improved internal controls can assist in controlling the adverse variances.

(4 marks)

BPP PRACTICE ASSESSMENT 2
LEVEL 4 SYNOPTIC ASSESSMENT

ANSWERS

Level 4 Synoptic Assessment
BPP practice assessment 2: answers

Task 1 (20 marks)

(a) The statutory duty to maintain a public record of information about SL Products Ltd is that of | Companies House | .

(2 marks)

(b)

	✓
Instruct Hina Khan to make an immediate bank transfer to Naseem	
Advise Jane Patel of the omission	✓
Prepare a journal to record Naseem's gross pay	
Write out a cheque for Naseem	

(2 marks)

(c)

Ten hours pay paid to J. Utley instead of T. Utley	Would not be detected
Gross pay credited to an expense account	Would be detected
Payment of PAYE to the pension administrator rather than HMRC	Would not be detected
Miscalculation of employer's National Insurance	Would not be detected
A transposition error in the net pay authority given to BACS	Would be detected

(5 marks)

(d)

	✓
System controls	
Physical access controls	
Integrity controls	✓

(2 marks)

(e)

Integrity

You must comply with IAS 2 *Inventories*

(4 marks)

(f)

Keypad entry to the accounting office	Physical access control
User access restrictions to areas of the accountancy software	Integrity control
Review of the log file for access of areas of the accountancy system by the Financial Director	System control

(3 marks)

(g)

	✓
Management have a wide span of control	
Structure is highly dependent on hierarchy	✓
Management do a wide variety of tasks within the organisation	
Management have a smaller team, with clear, strict boundaries and tasks set.	✓

(2 marks)

Task 2 (15 marks)

(a)

The objective of companies is to maximise profit so, at first sight, the decision to focus on the product which generates most profit seems quite sensible.

However the profit per unit is calculated after deducting the fixed overheads which have been allocated to each product. The allocation to individual products is inevitably arbitrary, as the overheads do not relate to a particular product type. We are not told how fixed overheads have been allocated to individual products, but a change in the method of overhead allocation could produce very different amounts for profit per unit.

A better decision-making rule is to try to maximise contribution, which is achieved by focussing on the product with the highest contribution per unit. Contribution per unit is selling price per unit minus variable costs. Each unit sold contributes this amount towards paying the fixed costs and maximising total contribution which will ultimately generate more profit regardless of how fixed costs are allocated.

The contribution per unit of the three products are £95 (£245 – £150), £92.50 (£225 – £132.50) and £115 (£230 – £115) respectively. This would suggest that, if Merville is to restrict production to one product, it should only produce and sell GG44.

However there are further issues to consider. If XC72 and FH54 are discontinued, then the fixed overheads allocated to those products would need to be covered elsewhere. Sales of GG44 would be expected to increase so presumably more overhead would be absorbed by these sales, but there may be implications for the total (absorption) costs of a variety of other products sold by Merville.

Also, it is not a given that customers would be happy to buy GG44 instead of XC72 and FH54. Just because these products are similar does not mean that they are identical, and GG44 sells for £5 more than FH54. Merville may lose more revenue (and therefore contribution) than it gains.

In conclusion, Merville should not rush into this decision as it may not be as straightforward as it first appears.

(7 marks)

(b)

> In situations where there is a limiting factor, such as labour in this case, the decision rule changes. Merville should aim to maximise contribution per unit of limiting factor, which in this case would be contribution per labour hour as this will in turn maximise profit.
>
> Cynthia should therefore calculate contribution per unit divided by number of hours of labour required to produce each unit. As we know labour is £15 per hour, this means that contributions per labour hour are £47.50 (£95/2), £61.70 (£92.50/1.5) and £38.30 (£115/3) respectively. This would suggest that, if Merville intends to pursue its one-product strategy, it should concentrate on FH54. As FH54 uses half the labour of GG44, Merville can produce twice as many of FH54 with the available labour.
>
> However the points made about overhead allocation and product substitution in a one-product strategy remain valid.

(8 marks)

Task 3 (15 marks)

(a)

Systemic weakness	No effect on reported profit ✓	Understatement of reported profit ✓	Overstatement of reported profit ✓
Omitting sales		✓	
Understating the allowance for doubtful debts			✓
Overstating assets	✓		
Understating expenses			✓
Writing off valid debts as irrecoverable		✓	
Undervaluation of inventory at the period end		✓	

(6 marks)

(b)

	✓
Physical controls	
Segregation of duties	✓
Management controls	
Supervisory controls	✓
Organisation	
Authorisation (approval) of transactions	✓
Arithmetic and bookkeeping checks	
Personnel controls	

(3 marks)

(c) **(i)** The chief accountant appears to have nothing to do with day-to-day payroll activities, only exercising a light level of management control by reviewing actual payroll costs against budget after payments to employees and HMRC have been processed. Errors or even fraud could easily take place in Jane Patel's work without any early warning system for SLP's management.

(ii) The lack of segregation of duties in the payroll system means that there are no day-to-day checks and balances on Jane Patel's work, so the company is wide open to both misappropriation and misstatement. Through collusion with others or acting alone, Jane could create fictitious employees, fail to remove leavers from the payroll, misreport hours to be paid, miscalculate gross pay and deductions, make recording and posting errors, and make over- or under-payments of net pay to employees.

(iii) The lack of authorisation of transactions means that intentional frauds or unintentional errors could pass unnoticed, and the company could pay for hours that have not been worked.

(6 marks)

Task 4 (15 marks)

(a)

The total direct material variance compares the **flexed budget cost** for materials with the **actual cost** incurred. The flexed budget is the total budgeted cost of materials for the actual production of 50,400 units. It is not useful simply to calculate the variance as £21,950 adverse by comparing the actual cost of £252,350 with the budgeted cost of £230,400, because the two figures are based on different volumes of activity.

Flexing the budget calculates the **quantity of materials** which we would expect to use to produce the **actual production** achieved. If 19,200 kgs are required to make 48,000 units then 0.4 kg is required to make 1 unit (19,200/48,000). To make 50400 units we therefore require 20,160 kgs (50,400 × 0.4 kg). We expect each kg to cost £12 (£230,400/19,200). Therefore we expect that making 50,400 units would require 20,160 kilograms at a cost of £12 per kilogram, that is £241,920.

We now compare the **flexed budget cost** of £241,920 with the **actual cost** (£252,350) to produce the total material variance of £10,430. This variance is adverse because the **actual cost was greater than the flexed budgeted cost**.

The total variance can be split into two elements:

- The variance due to the price paid per kilogram being different to what we expected. This is the material price variance.

- The variance due to the quantity of material used per unit of production being different to what we expected. This is the material usage variance.

The expected cost of the 20,600 kilograms used is £247,200 (20,600 × £12).

Price variance

We calculate the price variance by comparing the **actual cost** of the 20,600 kilograms (£252,350) with the **expected cost** (£247,200). The difference or variance is £5,150. This variance is adverse because the **actual cost is greater than the expected cost**.

Material usage variance

We calculate the material usage variance by calculating the quantity of materials which we would expect to use to produce the actual volume of production. 50,400 units were produced and the expected quantity of materials to make these units is 20,160 kilograms. If we compare this to the actual quantity used of 20,600 kilograms we get an adverse variance of 440 kilograms, since we used more than we expected. This needs to be **valued at the expected cost** of £12 per kilogram. The adverse usage variance is £5,280 (440 × £12). The usage variance is always valued at the expected cost (the standard cost) because the price variance has already been isolated.

Total materials variance

Together the materials price and usage variances reconcile back to the total materials variance. The price variance of £5,150 adverse plus the £5,280 adverse usage variance explains the total variance of £10,430.

(10 marks)

(b)

			£
Budgeted variable cost for actual production			182,820
Budgeted fixed cost			97,500
Total budgeted cost for actual production			280,320
Variance	Favourable £	Adverse £	
Direct materials price	3,090		
Direct materials usage	4,130		
Direct labour rate		6,050	
Direct labour efficiency		12,100	
Fixed overhead expenditure	1,200		
Fixed overhead volume			
Total variance	8,420	18,150	9,730
Actual cost of actual production			290,050

(5 marks)

Workings

Budgeted variable cost per unit = (£57,320 + £112,200)/5,100 units = £33.24

Budgeted variable cost for actual production = 5,500 units × £33.24 = £182,820

Total budgeted cost for actual production = £182,820 + £97,500 (fixed costs)

= £280,320

249

Direct labour efficiency variance

5,500 units should have taken (× 10,200/5,100 hours)	11,000 hrs
But did take	12,100 hrs
	1,100 hrs (A)
At standard rate (£112,200/10,200)	× £11.00
Efficiency variance	£12,100 (A)

Fixed overhead expenditure variance = £97,500 − £96,300 = £1,200. Actual £1,200 lower than budgeted, so favourable.

Task 5 (20 marks)

(a)

SL Products Ltd Scorecard	Year ended 31 Dec 20X3	Year ended 31 Dec 20X4
Profitability and gearing (correct to 1 dp):		
Gross profit %	26.4%	33.5 %
Operating profit %	1.5%	2.1 %
Return on capital employed	4.6%	7.1 %
Gearing	22.2%	13.9 %
Liquidity ratios (correct to 1 dp):		
Current ratio	1.8:1	1.8 :1
Acid test/quick ratio	0.8:1	0.8 :1
Working capital days (correct to nearest day):		
Inventory holding period	107 days	73 days
Trade receivables collection period	58 days	39 days
Trade payables payment period	94 days	71 days
Working capital cycle	71 days	41 days

(10 marks)

(b) Profitability

	✓
Profitability has improved due to improved sales and reduced costs.	✓
The profitability ratios have improved due to increased sales, but cost control is still a problem.	
The ratios give mixed messages. Some have improved and some have deteriorated. Further investigation is required.	

(2 marks)

Gearing

	✓
The reduced gearing ratio reflects that equity has partially replaced lending in the company's financial structure.	✓
The level of gearing is not related to the company's profitability.	
The increased gearing ratio shows that the company has become more risky.	

(2 marks)

Liquidity

	✓
Both ratios have deteriorated which indicates that the company is less solvent.	
Both ratios have improved, indicating there are no concerns about the company's liquidity or solvency.	
Comparing the liquidity ratios with last year's tells us little about the company's solvency.	✓

(2 marks)

Working capital

	✓
The longer working capital cycle indicates the company is insolvent.	
The shorter working capital cycle indicates the company has addressed some solvency issues that appeared in 20X3.	✓
The change in the working capital cycle requires urgent investigation.	

(2 marks)

Overall performance and position

	✓
The company has a new shareholder whose cash has been used to invest in improving profitability and reducing financial risk.	✓
Steady progress has been made in 20X4, but profitability has declined and the company remains risky.	
The company continues to perform badly and is in danger of insolvency.	

(2 marks)

Task 6 (15 marks)

(a)

Transaction stream	Risk	Control objective	Control activity
Payroll	Company is fined for non-compliance with PAYE regulations	Ensure all deductions have been properly calculated and authorised	Check calculation and authorisation of all deductions Maintain separate records for each employee Reconcile total pay and deductions in wages control account regularly
Sales	Company charges for goods in error and loses custom	Only invoice goods that have been sent out	Ask customers to sign despatch notes as proof of receipt Prepare sales invoices from signed despatch notes and sales orders.
Purchasing	Company pays more than once for the same goods and the supplier does not correct the mistake	Only pay for liabilities once	Record payments promptly in the cash book and ledger. Only pay supplier invoices that match checked GRNs

(6 marks)

(b)

> The key factor leading to the actual profit being higher than the originally budgeted profit is the increase in sales volume achieved. Actual sales were 80,000 units compared to an original budget of 74,200 units, an 8% increase. Also helping is an increase in the sales price achieved, budgeted to be £534,240/74,200 = £7.20 per unit, but actually achieved at £581,400/80,000 = £7.27, a 0.9% increase.
>
> The second reason for the higher than budgeted profit is the £10,000 favourable variance on premises costs. A second workshop was budgeted but the company has managed with one workshop, presumably because opening inventory of finished goods was sufficient to achieve sales of 80,000 units without producing more than 75,000 units in the year.
>
> Some costs, eg materials and labour, report adverse variances so tend to reduce the profit achieved. Others, eg administration, report a favourable variance so increase the profit achieved.
>
> However it is the favourable increase in sales volume and premises variances that are the main factors in explaining the increase in profit.

(5 marks)

(c)

> It is possible that there may have been errors in the prices charged by suppliers for materials and distribution. Internal controls over the use of price lists when ordering should be checked. There may have been errors in processing and recording purchases underlying the costs, or there may have been poor purchasing procedures so that the best deal on prices was not secured.
>
> As far as labour costs are concerned there may be operational reasons, such as the use of overtime, for the variance on labour costs. However, there may have been poor control of time, mis-recording of time, and deliberate or careless overpayment of employees. Authorisation and management controls over payroll costs should be reviewed.

(4 marks)

Company background and history

Rawhide plc is engaged in the design, development, manufacture and distribution of model railway products, toy cars and board games.

The company was set up fifty years ago by the Tennison family and became listed on the London Stock Exchange in 20X0.

Judith King, Managing Director, joined Rawhide plc mid-way through 20X5. Judith has extensive financial and managerial experience working for both plcs and private limited companies. She also has a strong track record in improving the performance of companies that are experiencing financial difficulties. The other directors have all previously worked within the manufacturing and retail sectors at a senior level.

Rawhide plc offers its products under three well-known brands: Bonanza (model railways), Robit (toy cars), and Probe (board games).

These are sold through the company's website and by independent stores and major retailers throughout the United Kingdom (UK) and overseas. 75% of the company's sales are to UK customers where the brand names have an iconic status. Rawhide plc has one major competitor in both the model railway and toy car markets – primarily due to the strength of the company's brands which make market entry costs highly prohibitive – and several smaller competitors in the board games market.

Rawhide plc's head office, manufacturing plant and distribution warehouse are all located in London. The model railway products and toy cars are manufactured by Rawhide plc in the UK, but the board games are produced by a third-party supplier located in India. These are then shipped back to the UK for onward distribution. In recent years the product range of the company has expanded significantly, with over 1,600 product lines now actively being managed.

Company performance

Rawhide plc has faced challenging trading conditions over the last couple of years. This is primarily due to a downturn in the global macro-economic environment in which the company operates and increased competition from the video games sector. Consumers have less money to spend on their hobbies and toys and there is a greater number of competing interests for this. Companies operating in the video games sector also typically have far higher marketing budgets than Rawhide plc can afford.

Rawhide plc's difficulties have also been compounded by supply chain and warehousing issues. The company does not enjoy an exclusive relationship with its Indian supplier. This has led to delays in introducing new products and meeting existing demand, as the supplier also has to satisfy the needs of other customers and only has a limited manufacturing capacity. There have also been problems with the stock control process in the UK warehouse, with high levels of stock building up for some product lines and stock-outs for others. This has had an

adverse impact on customer goodwill and a potentially harmful effect on the reputation of the brands upon which Rawhide plc greatly relies.

Rawhide plc reported lower revenues and profits for the year ending 31 December 20X4 and began to experience cash flow problems in the early part of 20X5. Ridley Nolan, the then Managing Director, resigned and was replaced by Judith King.

Upon her appointment, Judith immediately announced a major strategic review of all aspects of the business – in order to increase profits and improve cash generation – and sought additional equity funding and a revised overdraft facility to help support the working capital needs of the company and reassure creditors. Rawhide plc has yet to go overdrawn since issuing the shares.

Employees

Recruitment, development and retention of high quality staff are crucial to the success of any business. Rawhide plc employs 210 people in total (Production 70, Sales, Marketing and Distribution 106, and Administration 34). A number of designers and skilled craftsmen work in the Production department, which enables Rawhide plc to continually release innovative new products to the market. This allows them to remain contemporary and stay ahead of the competition, which is essential to preserve the status of its brands. Although Rawhide plc has continued to hire experienced professionals, it has had to cut its apprenticeship programme and curtail spending on certain training courses in order to save costs. The number of people employed in Sales, marketing and distribution has also fallen in recent years as the company has expanded its e-commerce platform.

Upon joining the company Judith King immediately implemented an annual UK employee survey to ascertain how Rawhide plc's employees felt about all aspects of their work. This included levels of workload, fair treatment in the work-place, management communications, and career path. She had used the questionnaire in the previous company she had worked for and found that it led to year-on- year improvement and a more positive and inclusive working environment. Staff turnover rates and levels of absenteeism have been markedly higher for Rawhide plc since the company first began to experience financial difficulties, and the survey confirmed that staff morale was poor, with many employees expressing concerns about their job security. An Equality and Diversity Committee has also now been set up, in response to the survey results, to build and form a culture within Rawhide plc that values difference in the workplace.

Customers

Customer loyalty, as measured by the number of repeat sales made to customers, reached a low point in the first six months of the year. As a consequence Rawhide plc has initiated an action plan to engage more with customers, principally through social media, for example discussion forums and blogs, and improve levels of customer service. Judith King believes that taking account of what customers think and how they feel will increase their sense of inclusion and thereby increase sales.

Given that a higher proportion of Rawhide plc's sales are now being made direct to customers through its website – following a decrease in the number of retail outlets selling their product on the high street

The company has also increased investment in its e-commerce operations to help ensure a smooth and positive customer experience.

Staff

Some of Rawhide plc's key personnel are listed below:

Managing Director	Judith King
Finance Director	Chris Burke
Production Director	Lech Polaski
Sales Director	Tanisha Prince
Financial Controller	Harry Archer
Purchasing Manager	Sheila Atim
Warehouse Manager	Bertie Carvel
Credit Controller	Kumail Sharif
Accounts Payable Clerk	Jemma May
Accounts Receivable Clerk	Robert Dobson
General Accounts Clerk and Cashier	Laura Wood
Payroll Clerk	John Mann

Rawhide plc's financial statements

The financial statements of Rawhide plc for the year ended 31 December 20X5 show that the company had a turnover of £62 million, and made a profit before tax of £2.2 million.

Rawhide plc – Statement of profit or loss for the year ended 31 December 20X5

Continuing operations	£000
Revenue	62,000
Cost of sales	(33,874)
Gross profit	28,126
Distribution costs	(15,922)
Administrative expenses	(9,634)
Profit from operations	2,570
Finance costs	(351)
Profit before tax	2,219
Tax	(427)
Profit for the period from continuing operations	1,792

Rawhide plc – Statement of financial position as at 31 December 20X5

	£000
ASSETS	
Non-current assets	
Property and equipment	6,718
Current assets	
Inventories	7,916
Trade receivables	11,465
Cash and cash equivalents	1,470
	20,851
Total assets	27,569

	£000
EQUITY AND LIABILITIES	
Equity	
Ordinary share capital (£1 shares)	1,000
Share premium	12,486
Retained earnings	4,651
Total equity	18,137
Non-current liabilities	
Bank loans	2,168
Current liabilities	
Trade payables	6,849
Tax liabilities	415
	7,264
Total liabilities	9,432
Total equity and liabilities	27,569

BPP PRACTICE ASSESSMENT 3
LEVEL 4 SYNOPTIC ASSESSMENT

Time allowed: 3 hours

PRACTICE ASSESSMENT 3

Level 4 Synoptic Assessment
BPP practice assessment 3

This practice assessment is based on the same scenario as AAT's live assessment, Rawhide. See pages 173–180 for the relevant pre-reading material.

Task 1 (20 marks)

(a)   Complete the following statement.

The fundamental qualitative characteristics that underlie the preparation of useful general purpose financial statements are [▼] and

[▼] .

Picklist:

accruals
faithful representation
going concern
relevance

(2 marks)

At Rawhide the task of preparing payment runs to suppliers and employees is performed by Laura Wood (General Accounts Clerk and Cashier). Harry Archer, the Chief Accountant, authorises each list of payments before Laura instructs the bank to make the payments by BACS. Because Harry is very busy working with the new Managing Director, Judith King, he has appointed the Production Director, Lech Polaski, to review the payments run. Lech has noticed that the amount of one payment to a major supplier is incorrect.

(b)   What is the appropriate action for Lech Polaski to take?

	✓
Instruct Chris Burke, the Finance Director, to apologise to the supplier	
Advise Laura Wood of the error in the payment	
Prepare a cheque to the supplier	
Write a memo to Judith King, the Managing Director	

(2 marks)

(c) Laura Wood, the General Accounts Clerk and Cashier, has asked you to show whether the following would be detected by preparing a bank reconciliation.

A payment was made to Hardacre Supplies rather than Harriman Supplies	▾
A cheque payment to Greenside & Co has not yet been banked by the supplier	▾
A transposition error was made when recording a receipt in the cash book	▾
A prompt payment discount was available but was not taken advantage of when paying Foxtrot Ltd	▾
A bank transfer was received by the bank but was omitted from the cash book	▾

Picklist:

Would be detected

Would not be detected

(5 marks)

You have recommended that, for each payroll run, a total of the number of personnel on the payroll should be automatically checked to ensure no unauthorised amendments have been made to Rawhide's payroll.

(d) Which type of control is this?

	✓
A programmed control over standing data	
A general IT control	
An authorisation check	

(1 mark)

Your duties at Rawhide include preparing the consolidated accounts. Harry Archer, the Chief Accountant, has instructed you to consolidate into the company's results a foreign associate and a foreign subsidiary that were acquired at different times during the year. Having asked you to start the consolidation on Monday, he tells you he expects it to be finished and ready for his review first thing on Tuesday. You have not covered foreign currency transactions or complex consolidations in your studies yet.

(e) Answer the following questions.

Which of your fundamental ethical principles is threatened by this request?

▼

Picklist:

Confidentiality
Objectivity
Professional competence and due care

What action should you take?

▼

Picklist:

You must comply with Harry's instruction as well as you can
You must request more time and assistance from Harry to complete the task
You must resign

(4 marks)

(f) Identify the MOST useful report required by the following stakeholders.

Potential new investors to the company	▼
Board of Directors	▼
HM Revenue & Customs	▼

Picklist:

Balanced Scorecard of the company
Corporation tax return for the period
Financial statements as filed with the Registrar of Companies
Statement of cash flows
Statement of financial position

(6 marks)

Task 2 (15 marks)

Judith King (Managing Director) has been reviewing the past budgets of Rawhide in preparation for future strategy planning. She has noticed that there are invariably adverse variances in the sales budget and favourable variances in the research and development budget even though actual performance in these areas has improved year on year. She has also noted that training spending is always much higher in the month of December than it is in the other months of the year. She is wondering whether these trends are due to behavioural factors.

(a) **Suggest why variances in the sales budget are invariably adverse, suggesting that staff are not attempting to meet the budgeted targets. In your answer, suggest how the situation could be improved.**

(4 marks)

(b) **Suggest why variances in the research and development budget are invariably favourable, and how the situation could be improved.**

(4 marks)

(c) **Suggest and explain reasons for why training expenditure is higher in December, at the financial year-end. Suggest how any change may improve Rawhide's performance.**

(3 marks)

(d) **Judith King is considering introducing performance related pay in Rawhide. Explain the elements that must be in place in order for this to motivate managers to achieve their targets.**

(4 marks)

Task 3 (15 marks)

Last year the adequacy of the controls over Rawhide's three main transaction streams were reviewed. Risks were identified. The Finance Director, Chris Burke, has asked you to advise on control objectives relating to the identified risks and also to recommend control activities to avoid or reduce these risks.

(a) **Identify ONE control objective and at least TWO control activities for each risk.**

Transaction stream	Risk	Control objective	Control activity
Payroll	The company overpays its employees.		
Sales	The company supplies goods to customers but customers do not pay for these goods.		
Purchasing	The company fails to pay for goods/services received resulting in the loss of suitable suppliers willing to trade with it.		

(6 marks)

As part of the review of the controls, Judith King, Managing Director, has been considering the risk of fraud in the business.

Judith King is concerned about the potential impact of fraud on the company.

(b) **List the THREE ways that fraud can impact upon a business.**

```



```

(3 marks)

You have been asked to review the adequacy of the control in Rawhide's accounting procedures. Your review has established the following information.

The company operates an integrated accounting system which includes a receipts and payments module. Harry Archer, the Chief Accountant, is responsible for managing cash book activities. Laura Wood, the General Accounts Clerk and Cashier, performs day-to-day cash book tasks.

Laura Wood's responsibilities include:

- Maintaining standing data on employee and supplier bank accounts

- Calculating payments to suppliers

- Recording payments from customers

- Calculating VAT on cash sales and purchases

- Recording discounts received from suppliers and discounts given to customers

- Preparing the cash book

- Authorising the BACS payments each month to employees and HMRC

- Reconciling the cash book to the bank account

Once a month Harry Archer compares total receipts and payments to budgeted receipts and payments, and investigates unexpected variances.

(c) **Which THREE of the following types of control activity are weakest in Rawhide's cash system?**

	✓
Personnel controls	
Management controls	
Supervisory controls	
Organisation	
Authorisation (approval) of transactions	
Physical controls	
Arithmetic and bookkeeping checks	
Segregation of duties	

(3 marks)

(d) **Explain THREE ways in which the weak control activities could create problems for the company.**

Note. You are **not** required to make recommendations to change procedures.

(i)

(ii)

(iii)

(3 marks)

Task 4 (15 marks)

You have been given the following information for the manufacture of units of HW by Rawhide for the month just ended.

	Budget		Actual	
Production (units of HW)		20,000		21,000
Direct labour	8,000 hours	£104,000	8,500 hours	£106,250

Chris Burke, the Finance Director, has asked you to write a note to help in the training of a junior accounting technician. The notes are to explain the calculation of the total direct labour variance and how this variance can be split into a rate variance and an efficiency variance.

(a) **Explain the total direct labour variance and how it can be split into a rate variance and an efficiency variance. Use calculations to illustrate your explanation.**

(9 marks)

Harry Archer, the chief accountant, has prepared the following budgetary control report for the product JC produced by Rawhide, together with the variances calculated below (though he has not specified whether each one is adverse or favourable).

	Budget		Actual	
Production (units)	2,125		2,250	
Direct materials	17,000 kg	£23,800	16,800 kg	£24,360
Direct labour	4,250 hours	£46,750	4,550 hours	£50,400
Fixed overheads		£61,000		£62,100
Total cost		£131,550		£136,860

Variances	Amount £
Direct materials price	840
Direct materials usage	1,680
Direct labour rate	350
Direct labour efficiency	550
Fixed overhead expenditure	1,100

Rawhide normally prepares an operating statement under standard absorption costing principles but Chris Burke, the Finance Director, has asked you to prepare an operating statement under standard marginal costing principles.

(b) **Place each variance into the correct column (favourable or adverse) and complete the table.**

			£
Budgeted variable cost for actual production			
Budgeted fixed cost			
Total budgeted cost for actual production			
Variance	Favourable £	Adverse £	
Direct materials price			
Direct materials usage			
Direct labour rate			
Direct labour efficiency			
Fixed overhead expenditure			
Fixed overhead volume			
Total variance			
Actual cost of actual production			

(6 marks)

Task 5 (20 marks)

Chris Burke, the Finance Director, is preparing a presentation for the board of directors. He has asked you to complete a comparative 'score card' of key financial ratios which he will use as part of his presentation.

Relevant data has been extracted from the last two years' accounts.

Extracts from accounts of Rawhide	Year ended 31 December 20X5 £000	Year ended 31 December 20X4 £000
Sales revenue	62,000	65,430
Cost of sales	(33,874)	(37,600)
Gross profit	**28,126**	**27,830**
Profit from operations	**2,570**	**945**
Assets		
Non-current assets	6,718	7,345
Inventories	7,916	6,448
Trade receivables	11,465	15,422
Cash and equivalents	1,470	72
Total	**27,569**	**29,287**
Equity and Liabilities		
Equity	18,137	16,924
Non-current liabilities	2,168	1,000
Trade payables	6,849	7,763
Bank overdraft	0	3,400
Tax liabilities	415	200
Total	**27,569**	**29,287**

(a) Complete the scorecard by calculating the missing ratios for the year ended 31 December 20X5.

Rawhide Scorecard	Year ended 31 December 20X5 £000	Year ended 31 December 20X4 £000
Profitability and gearing (correct to 1 dp):		
Gross profit %	45.4%	42.5%
Operating profit %	4.1%	1.4%
Return on capital employed		
Gearing		
Liquidity ratios (correct to 1 dp):		
Current ratio		
Acid test/quick ratio	1.8:1	1.3:1
Working capital days (correct to nearest day):		
Inventory holding period	85 days	63 days
Trade receivables collection period		86 days
Trade payables payment period		
Working capital cycle		

(10 marks)

(b) **Select the ONE correct observation about each aspect of business performance below.**

Profitability

	✓
The profitability ratios have improved due to more sales direct to customers rather than through wholesalers.	
Profitability has improved due to improved sales and reduced costs.	
Profitability has declined due to reduced sales and poor staff morale.	

(2 marks)

Gearing

	✓
The gearing ratio has improved due to the conversion of the bank overdraft to a bank loan.	
The level of gearing is mainly related to the company's profitability.	
The gearing ratio has worsened due to the conversion of the bank overdraft to a bank loan.	

(2 marks)

Liquidity

	✓
The company needs to review its finished inventory lines as there are too many and it is difficult to see what is causing the problem.	
Trade payable payment days need reviewing as suppliers are getting increasing delays in payments which will affect profitability.	
Cash flow has improved because of the conversion of the bank overdraft to a bank loan.	

(2 marks)

Working capital

	✓
The working capital cycle has improved suggesting improving controls.	
The improvement in trade receivables suggests credit control has improved year on year.	
The trade receivable collection period has worsened year on year, suggesting that the company is facing insolvency.	

(2 marks)

Overall performance and position

	✓
The company is technically insolvent.	
The company's profitability will have been worsened by converting the bank overdraft to a bank loan.	
The company has a new shareholder whose cash has been used to invest in improving profitability and reducing financial risk.	

(2 marks)

Task 6 (15 marks)

The additional following information has been provided.

Note. This part of the scenario will change in the live assessment, and is provided purely for practice.

The distribution warehouse and the manufacturing plant of the model railway products and toy cars are both in London. They are four miles apart, and the company uses a logistics company, Movelt Ltd, to transport the products from one site to the next. Movelt Ltd are a new logistics company for Rawhide, brought in during 20X5 as they offered a more competitive rate than the company used previously.

In respect of the model railways, once the production has been completed in the manufacturing plant for a specific run, the goods are packed onto a pallet ready for shipment to the distribution warehouse. The product bar codes are scanned and the accounting system recognises that these products are now 'in stock' and available for purchase by retailers or online customers. The pallets will remain in the despatch bay until Bertie Carvel, Warehouse Manager, arranges for Movelt to deliver the pallets to the distribution warehouse.

Sales orders:

- Customers can place orders online (both retail customers and wholesale customers) and once a sale has been generated, the order is sent automatically by the accounting system generating a sales order.

- The distribution warehouse staff unpack the pallet and put the products on the shelves which are marked up with a barcode. The barcode on the shelf is used by the warehouse staff to mark the location identification and to make finding the products easier when picking out orders.

Lech Polaski, the Productions Director, has an annual plan for production, and this is rolled out during the year. Due to its coverage on a popular television show 'Toys of Yesteryear', 20X5 saw one of the Rawhide products, a 1:80 replica of the 'Flying Scotsman', sell out within days. The previous Managing Director of Rawhide, Ridley Nolan, had been interviewed by the television crew a few months' earlier as Rawhide is one of the two leading manufacturers of model railways.

The production department has recently seen a high turnover of staff, particularly of the specialist craftsmen who hand paint the miniature trains and cars.

Inventory counts are completed once a year, just prior to the year end.

(a) **Identify THREE weaknesses in the Rawhide inventory system, and state a potential risk to the company as a result of this weakness.**

Weakness	Potential risks

(6 marks)

Judith King, the new Managing Director, has instructed Tanisha Prince, the Sales Director, to review her product portfolio. Tanisha has discovered that many products are relatively slow moving, but are specialist products which sell at a premium, due to the high quality of the craftsmanship involved.

	West Coast Highland (1:80)	R1166 Freight (1:80)	The Talisman (class A2) (1:80)	Total
Sale price	£340	£295	£280	
Sales for 20X5	150	400	1,255	
Variable costs	£123	£140	£167	
Fixed costs (allocated to the product line)	£17,000	£45,000	£120,000	£182,000

The following information is also available:

- It is proposed that either the West Coast Highland (WCH) or the R1166 is to cease production.

- This will allow resources to be diverted to The Talisman, which is growing in popularity as it is a replica of the model of train shown in a popular children's adventure film, 'May Bell and the Tasks of Doom'. Forecast sales of the train are expected to rise to 1,600.

(b) **Calculate the performance of the WCH and R1166 in terms of the profitability to the company. Complete the following table.**

	West Coast Highland (1:80) £	R1166 Freight (1:80) £	The Talisman (class A2) (1:80) £
Total sales value			351,400
Total variable costs			(209,585)
Total contribution			141,815

(4 marks)

(c) **Consider using calculations, the impact of the WCH ceasing production and The Talisman meeting the revised sales of 1,600 units**

(2 marks)

(d) **Consider using calculations, the impact of the R1166 ceasing production and The Talisman meeting the revised sales of 1,600 units**

(2 marks)

(e) **Conclude briefly which option management should take, support your answer with figures.**

(1 mark)

BPP PRACTICE ASSESSMENT 3
LEVEL 4 SYNOPTIC ASSESSMENT

ANSWERS

Level 4 Synoptic Assessment
BPP practice assessment 3: answers

Task 1 (20 marks)

(a) The fundamental qualitative characteristics that underlie the preparation of useful general purpose financial statements are ❘ relevance ❘ and ❘ faithful representation ❘.

(2 marks)

(b)

	✓
Instruct Chris Burke, the Finance Director, to apologise to the supplier	
Advise Laura Wood of the error in the payment	✓
Prepare a cheque to the supplier	
Write a memo to Judith King, the Managing Director	

The error needs to be corrected but the relevant parties informed.

Instruct Chris Burke, the Finance Director, to apologise to the supplier	Apart from it being not the best course of initial action here, it doesn't really solve the problem! The payments clerk wouldn't know that an error had been made and what action had been taken as the reviewer is going straight to the Financial Director to deal with it
Advise Laura Wood of the error in the payment	Correct as the payments team need to be aware of the error – then remedial action can be taken
Prepare a cheque to the supplier	No refunds can be made without authorisation. Also the payments team wouldn't have been made aware. Is this a true error? It will need confirmation from the payments team prior to any refund being issued.

Write a memo to Judith King, the Managing Director	This doesn't really solve the problem, just escalates the issue and the MD wouldn't be happy to be informed about every minor issue, this is where the department heads/directors should be involved. A memo to the payments director (Harry) copying in the payments team would be acceptable, if this was offered as an option.

(2 marks)

(c)

A payment was made to Hardacre Supplies rather than Harriman Supplies	Would not be detected
A cheque payment to Greenside & Co has not yet been banked by the supplier	Would be detected
A transposition error was made when recording a receipt in the cash book	Would be detected
A prompt payment discount was available but was not taken advantage of when paying Foxtrot Ltd	Would not be detected
A bank transfer was received by the bank but was omitted from the cash book	Would be detected

Reconciliations are checks where staff ensure that two different sources of information agree, and that any differences are understood. So for a bank reconciliation, the differences between the bank statement and the cash book are investigated.

Therefore, payments made to the wrong customer would not be detected as the payments would tally on both sources.

Missing a prompt payment discount would not be identified as, again, both the cash book and the bank statement would agree.

The other errors would be detected as there would be a difference on the bank statement and the cash book.

(2 marks)

(d)

	✓
A programmed control over standing data	✓
A general IT control	
An authorisation check	

This will be a specific programme designed for the payroll data only to be verified – this may be in the form of an activity log report to show the details behind any amendments, or a specific alert when changes are made. This is an example of an application control.

General IT controls would cover the overall IT system security such as use of passwords or access permissions.

An authorisation check would occur between a user making the change and the change being activated on the system (alternatively, if using paper authorisation, there may be authorisation prior to entering the data)

(1 mark)

(e)

Professional competence and due care

You must request more time and assistance from Harry to complete the task

(4 marks)

(f)

Potential new investors to the company	Financial statements as filed with the Registrar of Companies
Board of Directors	Balanced Scorecard of the company
HM Revenue & Customs	Corporation tax return for the period

Potential new investors would only have access to information available in the public domain, this would mainly be financial statements filed at Companies House. Share prospectus information may also be available for new listings, but this isn't an option here

HMRC are concerned with the tax information available from the company, so although they would also require a copy of the financial statements, it would be most useful for them to use the Corporation Tax information which specifically shows any deductions or allowances as well.

The Board of Directors would require different information regarding the performance of the company, available to those within the company. The balanced scorecard would enable them to see what areas are performing well, and the Board could request further information, such as cash flows, however, this is likely to be covered already, in more detail in the scorecard report.

(6 marks)

Task 2 (15 marks)

(a)

> An adverse sales variance suggests that the actual sales revenue achieved is lower than expected.
>
> The sales budget may be set consistently so high that staff consider it to be unachievable. Rather than motivating them to try harder it will have the opposite effect, in that they will become demotivated and deterred from trying their best.
>
> This is exacerbated if the sales budget includes items which are outside of sales staff control, for example if a policy by head office is imposed by someone other than the Sales Director whereby discounts are applied to bulk orders.
>
> In terms of motivation, the sales budget should be set at a level that is challenging yet attainable. This will be more likely if sales staff are involved in the budget setting process and have influence over the prices charged to clients.

[Tip: In your real assessment, you will be able to calculate ratios. If it is relevant to the question being asked (in this case, sales revenue and volume variances would be applicable) then use them to make your answer specific to the question and the scenario]

(4 marks)

(b)

> Favourable variances in the R&D department suggest that the actual costs incurred are lower than expected.
>
> If the variances in this department are consistently favourable, it may be that the managers are including budgetary slack in their estimates. They are therefore not spending their full budget allocation and so there appear to be achieving favourable variances.
>
> This is a problem because if all departments do this, the budgets will soon become unrealistic and meaningless. There will also be a temptation to spend up to the budget level when it is not necessary.
>
> To improve this situation, the directors should discuss the importance of accurate budgeting with their staff and get them to buy in to its importance. Staff should be reassured that if they exceed spending for good reason compared to the a more accurate budget then they will not be penalised.

[Tip: In your real assessment, you will be able to calculate ratios. If it is relevant to the question being asked (in this case, actual versus budgeted R&D expenditure variances would be applicable) then use them to make your answer specific to the question and the scenario]

(4 marks)

(c)

> There is a common phenomenon whereby people often believe that if they do not spend their budget in a particular year that the budget will be reduced in subsequent years, essentially a 'use it or lose it' approach. They may therefore spend money close to the year end on activities that do not offer great value to the company.
>
> Staff should be reassured that allowances in future years will not be cut if not used in the current year. Rawhide should consider allowing staff to rollover any unused amounts to the next year.
>
> With the staff morale being low, it would help Rawhide to boost this by encouraging a programme of training throughout the year, rather than in the busy season of December (Christmas orders).

(3 marks)

(d)

> Attractive potential rewards for staff: The rewards being offered by the performance related pay must be great enough to have an effect. If the potential rewards are small, then the motivating effect will be lost.
>
> Relevant to the   period: There should be a short timescale between the target being met and the reward being received, such as a financial year target, with the bonus being received within two to three months of the period end. This means that managers will have the reward in their sight and will try harder.
>
> Control: The staff who have the bonus should be able to influence and control the factors affecting their bonus. For example, a sale director should not be assessed on the materials wastage within production, as this is outside of their control. Instead, they could be assessed on an overall growth of 5% of revenue year on year.
>
> Long term aims of the company: Managers should be encouraged to buy in to the longer term goals of the company. This will improve their attitude to work generally and will also enhance the impact of the bonus.

(4 marks)

Task 3 (15 marks)

(a)

Transaction stream	Risk	Control objective	Control activity
Payroll	The company overpays its employees.	Only pay employees for work they have done **and** pay employees the amount authorised as shown in the agreed payroll listing. Ensure the standing data is accurate and up-to-date.	Time at work should be recorded using a 'clock in, clock out' system. Where employees are paid on an hourly basis, timesheets should be maintained. Refer to the standing data when calculating wages and salaries.

Transaction stream	Risk	Control objective	Control activity
			Payroll employees must update the standing data to reflect changes to pay rates, changes to overtime pay rates and non-statutory deductions from pay.
			Update payroll standing data to reflect changes in personnel.
Sales	The company supplies goods to customers but customers do not pay for these goods.	Only supply goods to customers who have been verified as having a good credit rating.	Credit terms should be authorised by senior personnel and reviewed regularly.
			Credit checks should be carried out on new customers prior to supplying to them.
			Changes to customer details recorded in the customer master file (for example, their address) should be authorised by senior personnel.
			Orders should only be accepted from customers where there is an expectation that they will pay the

Transaction stream	Risk	Control objective	Control activity
			amount due (ie no history of issues with receiving payment from them).
Purchasing	The company fails to pay for goods/services received resulting in the loss of suitable suppliers willing to trade with it.	Record all goods and services provided by suppliers.	Check purchase invoices are received for all goods received notes. Contact suppliers in the event of missing purchase invoices. Maintain a schedule of the date payment is expected to be made for each invoice. Reference invoices received with a sequential number so that the clerk is alerted to missing invoices due for payment.

A control objective is the correct action that should be taking place for example, for all sales made, a sales invoice should be raised. The control activity makes sure that the objective is met, for example, all despatch notes are agreed to sales orders and then agreed to sales invoices.

(6 marks)

(b)

> Financial: Fraud has a financial impact on the business as money and other assets are misappropriated. Also, the business may be liable for fines or penalties if it is found that that the company was negligent in not establishing appropriate procedures to prevent fraud.
>
> Reputation: The reputation of the company will be adversely affected both internally and externally. This may deter suppliers (or potential suppliers) from trading with the business.
>
> Employee morale: Employee morale can be affected if fraud is discovered and it may more difficult to recruit and retain high calibre staff in the future.

(3 marks)

(c)

	✓
Personnel controls	
Management controls	
Supervisory controls	✓
Organisation	
Authorisation (approval) of transactions	✓
Physical controls	
Arithmetic and bookkeeping checks	
Segregation of duties	✓

Supervisory – the definition of supervisory is a 'close oversight of people performing accounting tasks' (Course Book) – in this case, Laura's supervisor, Harry isn't closely supervising the payments run – he has delegated it to a director from a different department who is potentially unaware of the correct procedures (they are from the production department, so different altogether)

Authorisation – the definition of which is to 'ensure that only authorised personnel can make changes...authorise a bank payment' – the problem in the scenario is that Harry is the authoriser but he is delegating his task to another person – there is no indication that it is authorised, only that 'he is too busy'.

Segregation – Laura is both preparing and processing the payments – ideally these should be segregated roles.

Incorrect answers:

Management controls – definition of which is 'managers should review whether controls are being carried out' – not appropriate in this case, as no information is provided regarding what is completed after the payments have been made. Usually more 'past tense' and supervisory is more 'before the act'

Organisation controls – 'the way tasks and the business are organised as a whole' – again, not applicable to the question here – this doesn't question how the business is set up

Arithmetic and bookkeeping checks – otherwise known as accounting controls. Using accounting records to spot errors, such as out of balance TB, unreconciled items, reconciliations between sub ledgers and the TB. Again, not appropriate with payments to suppliers as the main issue in this scenario.

Physical controls – not appropriate in this scenario as no cash payments made, more aligned to physical inventory, cash, assets etc,

Personnel controls – are staff correctly trained and recruited for the correct role? Not the most appropriate answer for checking the payments being made to suppliers.

(3 marks)

(d) **(i)** The lack of **authorisation** of transactions means that intentional fraud or unintentional errors could pass unnoticed, and the company could pay a supplier twice, for instance, and subsequently fail to recover money belonging to the business.

(ii) The lack of **segregation of duties** in the cash book system means that there are no day-to-day checks and balances on Laura Wood's work, so the company is wide open to both misappropriation and misstatement. Through collusion with others or acting alone, Laura could create fictitious suppliers, transfer funds from the bank account to her own, miss opportunities to earn interest on deposits, teem and lade between accounts, miscalculate discounts and make over-or under-payments.

(iii) The chief accountant appears to have nothing to do with day-to-day cash book activities, only exercising a very light level of **management control** by reviewing actual payments and receipts at the end of each month. Errors and fraud could easily take place in Laura Wood's work without any early warning system for Rawhide's management.

(3 marks)

Task 4 (15 marks)

(a)

The total direct labour variance compares the **flexed budget cost** for labour with the **actual cost** incurred. The flexed budget is the total budgeted cost of labour for the actual production of 21,000 units. It is not useful simply to calculate the variance as £2,250 adverse by comparing the actual cost of £106,250 with the budgeted cost of £104,000, because the two figures are based on different volumes of activity.

Flexing the budget calculates the **quantity** of labour which we would expect to use to produce the **actual production** achieved. If 8,000 hours are required to make 20,000 units then 0.4 hours (24 minutes) is required to make 1 unit (8,000/20,000). To make 21,000 units we therefore require 8,400 hours (21,000 × 24 minutes). We expect each hour to cost £13 (£104,000/8,000). Therefore we expect that making 21,000 units would require 8,400 hours at a cost of £13 per hour, that is £109,200.

We now compare the **flexed budget cost** of £109,200 with the **actual cost** (£106,250) to produce the total labour variance of £2,950. This variance is favourable because the **actual cost was less than the flexed budgeted cost**.

The total variance can be split into two elements:

- The variance due to the rate paid per hour being different to what we expected. This is the labour rate variance.

- The variance due to the number of minutes used per unit of production being different to what we expected. This is the labour efficiency variance.

The expected cost of the 8,500 hours used is £110,500 (8,500 × £13).

We calculate the rate variance by comparing the **actual cost** of the 8,500 hours (£106,250) with the **expected cost** (£110,500). The difference or variance is £4,250. This variance is favourable because the **actual cost is less than the expected cost**.

We calculate the labour efficiency variance by calculating the number of hours which we would expect to use to produce the actual volume of production. 21,000 units were produced and these were expected to take 8,400 hours (21,000 × 0.4 hours). If we compare this to the actual hours used of 8,500 hours we get an adverse variance of 100 hours, since we took longer than we expected. This needs to be **valued at the expected cost** of £13 per hour. The adverse efficiency variance is £1,300 (100 × £13). The efficiency variance is always valued at the expected cost (the standard cost) because the rate variance has already been isolated.

Together the labour rate and efficiency variances reconcile back to the total labour variance. The rate variance of £4,250 favourable less the £1,300 adverse efficiency variance explains the total variance of £2,950 favourable.

(9 marks)

293

(b)

			£
Budgeted variable cost for actual production			74,700
Budgeted fixed cost			61,000
Total budgeted cost for actual production			135,700
Variance	**Favourable £**	**Adverse £**	
Direct materials price		840	
Direct materials usage	1,680		
Direct labour rate		350	
Direct labour efficiency		550	
Fixed overhead expenditure		1,100	
Fixed overhead volume			
Total variance	1,680	2,840	1,160
Actual cost of actual production			136,860

(6 marks)

Workings

Budgeted variable cost per unit = (£23,800 + £46,750)/2,125 units = £33.20

Budgeted variable cost for actual production = 2,250 units × £33.20 = £74,700

Total budgeted cost for actual production = £74,700 + £61,000 (fixed costs)

= £135,700

Each variance must be examined to decide if it is favourable or adverse. For example:

Direct labour efficiency variance

2,250 units should have taken (× 4,250/2,125 hours)	4,500 hrs
But did take	4,550 hrs
	50 hrs (A)
At standard rate (£46,750/4,250)	× £11.00
Efficiency variance	£550 (A)

Fixed overhead expenditure variance = £62,100 – £61,000 = £1,100. Actual £1,100 higher than budgeted, so adverse.

Task 5 (20 marks)

(a)

Rawhide Scorecard	Year ended 31 December 20X5 £000	Year ended 31 December 20X4 £000
Profitability and gearing (correct to 1 dp):		
Gross profit %	45.4%	42.5%
Operating profit %	4.1%	1.4%
Return on capital employed	12.7%	5.3%
Gearing	10.7%	5.6%
Liquidity ratios (correct to 1 dp):		
Current ratio	2.9:1	1.9:1
Acid test/quick ratio	1.8:1	1.4:1
Working capital days (correct to nearest day):		
Inventory holding period	85 days	63 days
Trade receivables collection period	67 days	86 days
Trade payables payment period	74 days	75 days
Working capital cycle	78 days	74 days

Workings

	Year ended 31 December 20X5 £000	Year ended 31 December 20X4 £000
ROCE $$\dfrac{\text{Profit from operations}}{\text{Total assets less current liabilities}}$$	$\dfrac{2,570}{27,569-6,849-415}$ **=12.7%**	$\dfrac{945}{29,287-7.763-3,400-200}$ **= 5.3%**
Quick Ratio $$\dfrac{\text{Current assets} - \text{inventory}}{\text{Current liabilities}}$$	$\dfrac{27,569-6,718-7,916}{6,849+415}$ **= 1.78:1**	$\dfrac{15,422+72}{7,763+3,400+200}$ **= 1.36:1**
Gearing $$\dfrac{\text{Non-current liabilities}}{\text{NCL + Equity}} \times 100$$	$\dfrac{2,168}{2,168+18,137}$ **= 10.7%**	$\dfrac{1,000}{1000+16,924}$ **= 5.6%**
Current Ratio $$\dfrac{\text{Current assets}}{\text{Current liabilities}}$$	$\dfrac{27,569-6,718}{7,264}$ **= 2.9:1**	$\dfrac{15,422+72+6,448}{11,363}$ **= 1.93:1**
Payable Days $$\dfrac{\text{Trade payables}}{\text{Cost of Sales}} \times 365$$	$\dfrac{6,849}{33,874} \times 365$ **= 73.8 days**	$\dfrac{7,763}{37,600} \times 365$ **= 75.4 days**
Working capital cycle	$85.3 + 67.5 - 73.8$ **= 78.5 days**	$62.6 + 86 - 75.4$ **= 73.2 days**

For a reminder on ratios, visit your *Financial Statements for Limited Companies* course book (Chapter 11).

(10 marks)

(b)　Profitability

	✓
The profitability ratios have improved due to more sales direct to customers rather than through wholesalers.	✓
Profitability has improved due to improved sales and reduced costs.	
Profitability has declined due to reduced sales and poor staff morale.	

Profitability has improved year on year (4.1% from 1.4% operating profit in the previous year). Retail sales make better profit margins than those to wholesalers.

(2 marks)

Gearing

	✓
The gearing ratio has improved due to the conversion of the bank overdraft to a bank loan.	
The level of gearing is mainly related to the company's profitability.	
The gearing ratio has worsened due to the conversion of the bank overdraft to a bank loan.	✓

The gearing ratio has worsened (10.7% from 5.6% in the previous year). We can see that the bank overdraft has reduced by £3.4 million, but the loan has increased by £1.168 million, suggesting that the company has taken out a loan in order to assist it's paying off of the overdraft.

Gearing is not connected to profitability, as gearing looks at the level of long term debt and a company can take out a long term loan, whilst still being profitable, perhaps with a view to expanding or investing in capital equipment.

(2 marks)

Liquidity

	✓
The company needs to review its finished inventory lines as there are too many and it is difficult to see what is causing the problem.	✓
Trade payable payment days need reviewing as suppliers are getting increasing delays in payments which will affect profitability.	
Cash flow has improved because of the conversion of the bank overdraft to a bank loan.	

Cash flow has deteriorated, not improved year on year if we use working capital cycle days as a guide (78 days up from 74 days in the previous year).

Trade payable days need reviewing, this is correct, however, the delays in payments affecting profitability are not relevant to looking at the liquidity of the company.

The scenario states that the company has a lot of different inventory lines which would be tricky to monitor the most profitable ones (if this was undertaken of course).

(2 marks)

Working capital

	✓
The working capital cycle has improved suggesting improving controls.	
The improvement in trade receivables suggests credit control has improved year on year.	✓
The trade receivable collection period has worsened year on year, suggesting that the company is facing insolvency.	

The working capital cycle has deteriorated, not improved.

There is an improvement in trade receivables (67 days down from 86 days in the previous period), suggesting an improvement in credit control.

(2 marks)

Overall performance and position

	✓
The company is technically insolvent.	
The company's profitability will have been worsened by converting the bank overdraft to a bank loan.	
The company has a new shareholder whose cash has been used to invest in improving profitability and reducing financial risk.	✓

The company is solvent. The company's new shareholder has been injecting cash into the business to improve profitability. The company's profitability has improved, not worsened year on year.

(2 marks)

Task 6 (15 marks)

(a) **Note.** Only three weaknesses and risks are required.

Weakness	Potential risks
The trigger for moving the completed inventory to the distribution warehouse seems to be driven by the space available in the despatch area. This means that the distribution warehouse will not have the goods, but the accounting system is showing the product as 'in stock'.	Loss of customer goodwill when the goods cannot be located by the distribution warehouse staff and the sale is cancelled by the customer service team. Loss of sale, and build-up of inventory levels.
There appears to be no method for identifying slow moving or fast moving inventory.	This can result in poor stock control, with a regular loss of sales due to incorrect inventory information, and overstocking on the slow moving items.
There is an annual budget of production runs, with no flexing according to the popularity of items or level of inventory already in place. This was demonstrated by the lack of flexibility of the production plan regarding the Flying Scotsman toy.	Loss of potential sales and customer goodwill.
A high turnover of staff, including in the warehouse, can mean staff are undertrained or very new to the company which may make identification of the specialist products more difficult during inventory counts.	Incorrect valuation of the inventory during inventory count by incorrectly identifying the product.
Low morale among staff, particularly in the production department, may result in poor quality products being produced.	Poor quality products will affect profit margins and may lose customers in the long term.
Increase in absenteeism will affect production schedules, and can result in delays on the production schedule with backorders building up.	Loss of sales and customer goodwill.

(6 marks)

(b)

	West Coast Highland (1:80) £	R1166 Freight (1:80) £	The Talisman (class A2) (1:80) £
Total sales value	51,000	118,000	351,400
Total variable costs	(18,450)	(56,000)	(209,585)
Total contribution	32,550	62,000	141,815

(4 marks)

(c) If the WCH ceases production to be replaced by additional Talisman sales, the overall impact will be an increase in contribution.

Workings

	£
Lost contribution from ceasing WCH (working to part (b))	(32,550)
Increased contribution from the additional Talisman sales: £141,815/1,255 × (1600 – 1,255) =	38,985
Net contribution change	6,435

(2 marks)

(d) If the R1 166 ceases production, with the Talisman increasing in sales, the overall impact will be a decrease in the contribution to the costs of the company.

Workings

	£
Lost contribution from ceasing R1166 (working to part (b))	(62,000)
Increased contribution from the additional Talisman sales: £141,815/1,255 × (1600 – 1,255) =	38,985
Net contribution change	(23,015)

(2 marks)

(e)

Management should cease production of the WCH as this is net positive contribution to the company of £6,435, whereas, ceasing the R1166 will result in a net reduction in contribution of £23,015.

In both cases, the fixed costs are not taken into account as marginal costing has been used to assess the viability of these three products.

(1 mark)